FEASIBLE PLANNING FOR
SOCIAL CHANGE

FEASIBLE PLANNING
FOR
SOCIAL CHANGE

by

Robert Morris and Robert H. Binstock

with the collaboration of

Martin Rein

COLUMBIA UNIVERSITY PRESS

NEW YORK AND LONDON, 1966

Robert Morris, Professor of Social Planning, the Florence Heller Graduate School for Advanced Studies in Social Welfare, at Brandeis University, is editor of *Social Work*, a consultant to numerous federal and voluntary organizations, and principal investigator for research projects funded by the Ford Foundation, the U.S. Public Health Service, and other agencies.

Robert H. Binstock, a political scientist, is an assistant professor at the Florence Heller Graduate School for Advanced Studies in Social Welfare and a consultant to various social welfare programs.

Martin Rein is Associate Professor, Carola Woerishoffer Graduate Department of Social Work and Social Research, Bryn Mawr College.

To
The Florence Heller Graduate School
for Advanced Studies in Social Welfare,
its Dean and Faculty,
for its environment of critical inquiry

PREFACE

A major premise of this book is that, at this time, discussions of "planning" need to be somewhat circumscribed if they are to be useful. The word currently connotes so many different kinds of individual and collective thoughts and actions that attempts to deal conceptually with the entire range of phenomena have resulted in considerable confusion. In man's twentieth-century attempts to cope with conditions of his existence he has developed sophisticated techniques for acquiring information about himself and his environment. But development of equally sophisticated concepts for the application of this information through planning has been hampered by a common tendency to discuss several types of planning as if they were indistinguishable in basic character. As a consequence, the simple generic term for rational problem-solving (planning) is now used in such varied contexts that it tends to hinder rather than aid communication. It seems to be the time to single out for consideration some of the major types of planning, in turn, in order to reduce confusion.

Although we were drawn together by our interests in many kinds of planning, it quickly became evident that we wished to say more about some aspects of planning than others. Moreover, we soon developed a conviction that our desire to communicate required us to make at least four decisions to facilitate a relatively systematic presentation.

As the title indicates, the first of our major decisions was to concentrate upon factors that determine the feasibility of planning goals and upon ways of revising unfeasible goals to make them feasible. We are not concerned about feasible goals *per se*, but about their role in maximizing achievements while minimizing waste of precious human and material resources for planning. Other aspects of planning, such as strategies for achieving feasible goals, are also discussed; but for the most part these are included either because they provide the necessary context for considering feasibility or because they indicate some of the rewards of understanding feasibility.

Second, we chose to focus attention on planning goals that embody a proposal for changing the policy of one or more organizations. This choice gives some analytical consistency to our description of goals. While it eliminates from consideration some activities that customarily fall under the heading of "social planning," it hardly confines our discussion to a unique or even a limited context. We believe that what we have to say is relevant to planning undertaken through public as well as private auspices, by city planners as well as social planners, for changing conditions of health, employment, education, income, recreation, housing, land use, and other dimensions of individual and collective existence.

A third decision was to present much of our discussion from a single viewpoint, that of "the planner." Sometimes the planner is an individual, employed by an organization; at other times, a formal or informal group which, to some degree, is united by a common purpose. This viewpoint may not be the most useful for comprehending the broad economic, social, and political forces that lead to societal or community change, but, within this larger context, it has proved to be quite helpful for understanding the opportunities for making an impact that are available to individuals engaged in planning.

A fourth decision was to raise a great many issues but not attempt to explore all of them exhaustively. The overriding purpose is to present a framework for approaching an understanding of planning, without yielding to the temptation to give disproportionate space to pet subjects or ideas. This book is intended to serve as an outline. We hope that we can expand it soon and that others will find it to be a useful foundation.

These choices were partially influenced by an opportunity to analyze a national demonstration program in community organization for the elderly, financed by the Ford Foundation. In 1960 the Foundation granted funds to five private organizations and two public agencies in various parts of the country so that each could employ a full-time staff member (a project director) to devote three years to planning programs and services for older persons. An additional grant was made to the Florence Heller Graduate School for Advanced Studies in Social Welfare, Brandeis University, for coordinating and studying the seven projects. This opportunity for research did much to stimulate and clarify our thinking.

While the material presented in this book is based to some extent upon interpretations of events in the demonstration projects, it cannot be regarded as an evaluative report in the conventional sense. Data from the Ford program are used more to illustrate our ideas than to document "findings." Additional works, some already published and others currently in preparation, report on the projects more fully. (Indeed, only four of the seven projects are discussed at any length here.) Readers already familiar with the details of the projects will find that in most instances a project director is called "the planner." In some of the illustrations, however, in order to avoid tedious presentations, we have used that term to refer to an employee of the organization sponsoring the project who played a more prominent role than the project director in staffing a particular planning effort.

The principal investigator for the over-all demonstration-research program was Robert Morris, of the Florence Heller

Graduate School for Advanced Studies in Social Welfare at Brandeis University. Although the seven organizations sponsoring the demonstrations were virtually autonomous in conducting their projects, Morris was responsible for establishing a general framework for studying developments in each community. He also initiated the systematic collection of data from project directors and other sources in the demonstration communities, and guided several early studies conducted through field visits by part-time research staff. A series of conferences on the Brandeis campus brought together the project directors, other representatives of the sponsoring organizations, and expert consultants to share experiences and to arrange the basis for Brandeis's research participation. These meetings were not used to help local representatives explore their planning problems, nor to provide them with expert consultation. While contact with the Brandeis research staff undoubtedly had some general effect upon the demonstration project staffs, every effort was made to limit this influence to those conditions necessary for collecting and reporting data, without encroaching on local decisions.

Robert Binstock joined the research staff in the third year of the program to administer data analysis. Eventually, he became an equal partner in all administrative, evaluative, and writing stages, with the major task of searching out coherent strands in the wealth of operational reports provided by each project. We found that our respective disciplines, social work and political science, made for a fruitful partnership.

Martin Rein, Associate Professor, the Carola Woerishoffer Graduate Department of Social Work and Social Research, Bryn Mawr College, began his association with the Ford program when he was a research associate at the Heller School. He contributed to early thinking about the subject and served as a periodic consultant after joining the Bryn Mawr faculty. He assumed responsibility for preparing initial drafts of two chapters, materials adapted for use in the final version. He also participated in the discussion preceding the final organization of the manuscript, undertook critical readings of several drafts, and provided valuable suggestions at all stages of development.

We have incurred many debts in producing this book. The Ford Foundation and Brandeis University provided financial and less tangible forms of support that made it possible to gather information, to think, and to write. The National Council on the Aging, United Community Funds and Councils of America, and various subdivisions of the United States Department of Health, Education, and Welfare were helpful in a number of ways. Cooperation from the United Community Fund of San Francisco, the Contra Costa Council of Community Services, the Metropolitan Council for Community Service (Denver), the Senior Citizens' Council of Metropolitan Denver, and the Community Services of Greater Worcester enabled us to obtain much of the project data appearing in these pages. We are also indebted to the sponsors of the other Ford projects: the Governor's Citizens' Council on Aging of Minnesota, the Golden Years, Inc., of Marion County, Kansas, the Kansas State Department of Social Welfare, and the Health and Welfare Council of Metropolitan St. Louis. Gratitude is due to the executives and staff members of these organizations and to the officers and members of each project committee. Individuals involved in the demonstration project, who helped in one way or another, are too numerous to record, but deserve our thanks.

We are grateful to the following publishers for permission to quote copyrighted material: the Macmillan Company for quotations from Edward C. Banfield's *Political Influence* (1961); Harcourt, Brace & World, Inc., for quotations from Karl Mannheim's *Man and Society in an Age of Reconstruction* (1940); the International Conference of Social Work, Inc., for quotations from "Social Progress through Social Planning: the Role of Social Work," Report of the Pre-Conference Working Party to the Twelfth International Conference of Social Work (1965); Columbia University Press for quotations from the National Conference on Social Welfare's *The Social Welfare Forum, 1963* (1963).

We are especially indebted to Ollie A. Randall, consultant to the Ford Foundation. Her encouragement, her advice, and her insights are priceless resources.

Howard Gustafson, President of the National Association of Social Workers, and Garson Meyer, President of the National Council on the Aging, are also due much thanks. Their consultation and site visits enriched our understanding of the planning that took place in the Ford projects.

Arthur Jette, Associate Director of the Research and Statistics Division, United Community Funds and Councils of America, and Jerry Solon, then Director of the Medical Care Studies Unit at Beth Israel Hospital, Boston, served on a technical consultation panel and gave valuable advice and criticism for the development of an initial plan for data collection. A specially commissioned study undertaken by Sanford Kravitz, then a doctoral student at the Heller School, provided information on the hundreds of persons who served on committees of the various organizations that sponsored the Ford projects. Other doctoral candidates who shared in the work for brief intervals were: William Denham, Ray Koleski, Melvin Mogulof, Bernard Olshansky, and Walter Stern. Elma Denham assisted with preliminary analyses of data.

Nothing would have been possible without the dedicated interest, full and intelligent reporting, and enthusiastic support of the persons who at one time or another served as project directors in the Ford demonstrations: William Bell, Gerald Bloedow, Aleta Brownlee, Gertrude Hall, Robert Linstrom, Helene Lipscomb, Elizabeth Reznicek, Richard Steinman, and

Esther Twente. Their willingness to shoulder the added burden of reporting to the Brandeis research staff, and their readiness to expose their actions to public scrutiny, made them unusually gratifying collaborators.

The following persons read a revised draft and provided us with thoughtful criticisms: Herbert Aptekar, Arnold Gurin, Edward Newman, Robert Perlman, Violet Sieder, and Roland Warren. Their suggestions enabled us to improve the manuscript; we are to blame for the faults that remain.

Helen Beck, Barbara Isaacson, Gwendoline Whateley, and our wives patiently helped us through a variety of disagreeable but indispensable steps. Dorothy Swart of Columbia University Press managed, somehow, to make this volume readable.

ROBERT MORRIS
Rome, Italy
ROBERT H. BINSTOCK
Waltham, Massachusetts

January, 1966

CONTENTS

I.   What Is Planning?   3

II. The Anatomy of Feasibility   25

III. Experiences in Social Planning   32

IV. The Dynamics of Goal Development   80

V.   Organizational Resistance to Planning Goals   94

VI. Overcoming Resistance through Influence   113

VII. Evaluating the Feasibility of Goals   128

VIII. Beyond Feasibility   150

     Bibliography   159

     Index   165

FEASIBLE PLANNING FOR
SOCIAL CHANGE

I · WHAT IS PLANNING?

This book is an attempt to comprehend the attempts of a single actor, possessing limited influence, to change the policies of formal organizations in order to improve conditions of social welfare. Such efforts have been varyingly termed "community organization," "politics," "civic education," and "social action." [1] We regard them as one of the more important facets of *social planning*.

At one time it was widely asked whether it is possible or desirable to plan changes in social conditions. There has been doubt about whether available technical knowledge is adequate for conscious ordering of the infinitely complex relationships among many millions of persons and many thousands of organizations. There has been fear that planning may lead to the tyranny of an elite. In recent years massive attempts to plan social change have been undertaken. Nations seek to guide and accelerate their economic and social growth. Governments in all parts of the world try to shape the design, functions, and growth of urban communities. Governments and industries plan vocational education to suit the labor requirements of rapidly changing economies. And, at least in the United States, government plans in order to reduce the incidence of mental ill-health, economic dependency, and juvenile delinquency.

[1] See Ross, *Community Organization;* Rossi and Dentler, *The Politics of Urban Renewal;* Peterson, *The Day of the Mugwump;* and Wickenden, "Social Action," *Encyclopedia of Social Work,* pp. 697–703.

Nevertheless, doubts of a serious nature remain about man's capacity to deal with social needs and relations through planning. Questions remain as to whether planning can be made more scientific, systematic, and effective. Most of those who are engaged in planning believe that it is in large part an art, compounded of experience, common sense, and professional expertness in a given realm of human affairs. Attempts to refine this art could conceivably be undertaken through logical analysis, large-scale surveys of practice, and comparative studies of planning in a variety of fields. But such attempts have been limited, for the most part, to intensive study of a single planning episode. They have tended to illuminate the distinctive and the idiosyncratic without producing useful generalizations. There are also reports about planning in economically underdeveloped countries, but their relevance to planning activities in highly developed industrial and urban settings, where a complex of organizations for handling social problems already exists, is limited.

In order to enhance our capacity to plan we need to identify elements which are common to a great number of planning activities and provide a basis for conceptual generalization. Without this the foundation is lacking for the sophisticated skills needed to cope with the social problems of today and tomorrow. The framework indicated in the first paragraph of this chapter is a suggested approach to meeting this need.

The thoughtful reader will already expect answers to a number of questions posed by our frame of reference. What is meant by a "single actor"? How limited is "limited influence"? Can one distinguish the policies of formal organizations well enough to detect what would and would not be a "change" in policy? Can any standards be used to judge what is an "improvement" in conditions of social welfare? What is "social welfare"? Indeed, what is "planning"?

"Planning," as commonly understood, presents few conceptual difficulties. Planning is a relatively systematic method which men use to solve problems. We call those who use this method "planners." When planners have identified what they would regard as a solution to their problem, we call that a "goal." Both the efforts of planners to identify goals and their attempts to achieve identified goals are called "planning." And, since the postulation of a problem implicitly indicates that the planner is dissatisfied with a current or an anticipated state of affairs, we generally regard planning as a method of intervention.

In our everyday usage of the term we connote the attempts of individuals, families, or small groups to solve problems; we speak of "planning menus" and "planning vacations." In more technical usage we are concerned with activity undertaken by collectivities—public agencies, commercial and industrial and eleemosynary organizations, communities, and nation-states; we speak of "planning programs," "planning services," "planning expansion," "planning cities," "planning economies." In both usages "planning" is a generic term for human endeavors to solve problems. In all instances we understand that the "planner" (who might be an individual or an organization—Mrs. Smith, the Joneses, the Denver Metropolitan Council for Community Service, the Chicago Public Housing Authority, General Motors, the Atomic Energy Commission) intends to bring about a change, that is, something different from what he would expect if he did not intervene in the course of events. Thus, Dahl and Lindblom define planning as "an attempt at rationally calculated action to achieve a goal." [2] And central planning is defined by Wilson as "a significant alteration in a community's state of affairs in accordance with the ends of some central agency that has a capacity to select those ends and the means for their attainment." [3]

[2] Dahl and Lindblom, *Politics, Economics, and Welfare,* p. 20.
[3] Wilson, "An Overview of Theories of Planned Change," in Morris, ed., *Centrally Planned Change,* p. 13.

However, when we attempt to transform this everyday term into a more exact definition that will include the kinds of actors, the kinds of problems, and the variables, it is a formidable task. For example, consider the incredible variety and contradictions in the federal government's definitions of social planning, summarized in a review of governmental planning for health and welfare:

1. ". . . the process by which a state or community orders the steps toward specific goals."
2. ". . . providing leadership and/or participating with other community agencies, organizations, and interested citizens in the development and/or extension of the broad range of resources and facilities to meet the social and economic needs of the community."
3. ". . . the state level coordinating group" [without administrative responsibility]; [the same federal bureau also states that] ". . . any organization or agency that presumes to coordinate activities or services, without itself administering such services, cannot really 'coordinate.'"
4. . . . the process "to derive solutions to socially recognized problems" . . . [by] constructing a theoretical explanation, converting it into programs, devising operations, and finally evaluating . . .[4]

Frequently, social planning is simply conceptualized as a series of discrete steps. For example, the Twelfth International Conference of Social Work (1964) dealt with the subject in the following terms:

The steps taken in planning may be briefly enumerated as follows:
 i) description, based on different data . . .
 ii) choice of objectives, which implies the will to change the natural course of evolution.
iii) arbitration between selected objectives—determination of an order of preference or priority . . .

[4] The material within quotation marks is quoted from various sources by Schottland, "Federal Planning for Health and Welfare," in *The Social Welfare Forum, 1963*, pp. 109–10; the numbers are supplied by the present authors.

iv) determination of ways of action: search for the best route, consideration of steps to be taken, timetable, conditions in which means and resources are put into operation.

v) guidance and control of physical or final execution and especially coordination of tasks . . .

vi) evaluation of results . . .[5]

The Conference also emphasized the absolute necessity, as a general prerequisite for all steps in social planning, of

the widest possible participation of individuals, groups, organizations, local and national bodies . . . appropriate consultative procedures and bodies at different levels in the nation and at different levels in the elaboration of a plan . . . for preserving freedom and democracy . . . preventing usurpation of power by the planners . . . [and for bringing to bear] . . . relevant information . . .[6]

While it may not be possible to find a neat and compact definition of social planning, and it may be difficult to formulate one with which everyone will agree, it is possible to isolate several elements which characterize the term "planning" and which can provide a framework for analysis without violating common understanding of the term.

The relatively informed quality of the planner's intervention is one factor that leads us to distinguish planning from other methods of solving problems.[7] Any attempt to solve a problem requires choices among alternatives. When these choices are based on "the flip of a coin," "the whim of the moment," "the dictates of custom," or "blind faith," we call them "arbitrary," "impulsive," "unimaginative," or "uninformed." When we speak of planning, we assume that at least some of these choices are

[5] "Social Progress through Social Planning: the Role of Social Work," Report of the Pre-Conference Working Party to the Twelfth International Conference of Social Work (Chalkis, Greece: International Conference of Social Work, 1965), p. 13.

[6] *Ibid.*, p. 16.

[7] Some of the other methods of problem-solving frequently identified in common usage are: trial and error; arbitrary selection; custom, habit, or prescription; hunch, intuition, or sixth sense; and chance or accidental discovery. For an exhaustive discussion of methods for solving problems see Braybrooke and Lindblom, *A Strategy of Decision: Policy Evaluation as a Social Process.*

guided by knowledge of the dynamic relationships between a given problem and alternative solutions to it—an understanding of cause and effect, action and reaction, and means and end. It is the use of this understanding to which we refer when we describe planning as a "rational" method of solving problems.

Moreover, because this knowledge sometimes makes it possible to develop a relatively detailed prediction of the likely consequences of considered actions and events, we also assume that planning is superior to other methods. Our respect for this prediction, which we call a "plan," leads us to regard the theoretical function of planning as "effective problem-solving." [8]

Most discussions of planning convey far more than the notion that the function of planning is effective problem-solving. Any given usage of the term implies that the planner is attempting to control certain specified variables. Planning to increase family savings is at least concerned with such matters as income, consumption patterns, taxes, and interest rates. City planning is at least concerned with zoning, subdivision, building codes, esthetics, transportation, and special project or land-use developments. Similarly, the planning of national economies, vacations, homemaker services, mental health facilities —all distinguishable types of planning and techniques of

[8] Our common understanding of the distinction between planning and other methods of solving problems corresponds to Mannheim's distinction between *Erfinden* (invention) and *Finden* (chance discovery)—advanced and primitive stages in the development of human thinking. In the primitive stage (*Finden*), "some individual or group discovers accidentally, among a very large number of possibilities, the kinds of reaction which fit a given situation. The achievement of thought then lies in remembering the correct solution which has been discovered."

In order to attain a more advanced stage of thinking (*Erfinden*), "man had to imagine a definite goal and then think out in advance how to distribute his activities in a given way over a certain period of time with this goal in view. He did not in such cases have to think beyond the task immediately at hand. But he had at least to be able to imagine how the object of his thought fitted into the immediate environment. He had also to be able to foresee the most probable consequences of an event." Mannheim, *Man and Society in an Age of Reconstruction*, pp. 150–51.

control—involves a relatively unique configuration of variables.

It is because of, rather than in spite of, these different sets of specified variables that we call all these planning. For by common definition the planning method can be used to solve problems only when the planner understands the nature of the problem and the relation to it of alternative solutions. It is not sufficient for a planner to predict that certain actions will lead to certain reactions; he must be able to grasp the relationship theoretically. He must be able to explain his predictions as to the relative merit of alternative solutions and the means for achieving them.[9] Each kind of planning involves the attempts of certain kinds of actors to solve certain kinds of problems, using an understanding of the dynamic relationships among sets of relevant variables.

The conceptual confusion which has plagued efforts to comprehend social planning is symptomatic of a more general problem associated with the mid-twentieth-century struggles of man to cope with the developments of increasingly complex industrial societies. Expanding population, increased longevity, urbanization, and automation have posed a number of unfamiliar problems. They are problems which we have determined more and more to take up collectively.

Consider, for example, the new attention given by government and voluntary organizations to the needs of the elderly. Sixty years ago a relatively small proportion of the adult population was over seventy years of age, and the needs of this number could be met by their families, supplemented by small-scale philanthropic or church assistance. But improved economic status, better health, and various medical advances have resulted in a very great increase in the proportion of adults in

[9] As Bell notes: "Only with an adequate explanation—an understanding of relevant variables—can one seek to control or transform a situation. Conjecture, in this sense, stipulates a set of future predicates whose appearance should be explainable from theory. Prediction without explanation is insight, experience, or luck." Bell, "Twelve Modes of Prediction," *Dædalus,* XCIII (1964), 846–47.

the total population who survive into their seventies, eighties, and nineties. Since our industrial society does not require the labor of most of these persons, retirement at sixty or sixty-five is commonplace. Individuals withdrawn from the labor force experience a sharp reduction in income which places many of them below the level of poverty despite the productiveness of their earlier adult years. For most of them the purchase of adequate medical care, or the maintenance of health through sound nutrition and proper medical attention, is financially impossible. Despite the general improvement of health among the aged, large numbers do, in time, suffer from chronic illnesses which require special care and medical treatment over long periods of time. Moreover, the fact that between 10 percent and 15 percent of the population exists without visible social purpose produces a serious human as well as social problem in many communities: what, for these retired persons, is the purpose of living?

Many corrective measures have been undertaken to cope with these problems. Older persons organize themselves into senior citizens' groups in an attempt to improve their own situations. National policies have affected employment of older workers and have continually adjusted those portions of the national income distributed to the elderly through governmental mechanisms. Income is provided through a national compulsory retirement insurance system (a policy reinforced by labor-management contracts). Housing at low rentals is made available in many parts of the country. Attempts are made to develop home-care services for the chronically ill through programs which can guarantee necessary supports in the volume and variety required. Extended care is provided in nursing homes and homes for the aged. Educational programs are stimulated to prepare older adults to adjust to retirement; community activities are launched to fill empty hours and to encourage the participation of the aged in civic affairs. Personnel are trained to staff most of these programs.

As we have accepted the challenge of solving such problems, we have tried to make use of our most modern method for doing so—planning. But the application of the planning method to these problems is not easily accomplished. The problems posed by an advanced industrial society are not only unfamiliar but sufficiently strange in kind and degree of complexity to constitute almost a new genus of problem. We are reaching a stage in the development of thought and action in which problems and goals which we formerly comprehended in relative isolation are perceived in complex, interdependent relationships. Unemployment is currently seen, for example, as in some degree a function of tax rates, interest rates, consumption, savings, investment, the wage-price spiral, balance of trade, education and training, segregation, immigration, and automation. In turn, unemployment is viewed as a factor that affects each of these. In our emergent state of social awareness it is not surprising that the phrase "multifaceted problem" has become hackneyed. As Karl Mannheim expresses it:

The tensions which underlie our conscious goals . . . are gradually compelling us to pass on to another stage . . . when man and society advance from the deliberate invention of single objects or institutions to the deliberate regulation and intelligent mastery of the relationships between these objects.[10]

Our ambition to deal with these complex phenomena by planning—to control and modify these situations in accordance with specified ends—demands more extensive knowledge and more sophisticated techniques and thought processes than ever before. It is difficult enough to specify the problems. To comprehend the means-end, cause-effect, action-reaction relation-

[10] Mannheim, *op. cit.*, p. 152.

ships of the relevant variables to alternative solutions is formidable. Moreover, since these problems are identified to greater and lesser degrees (sometimes not at all) as collective problems, the identity of the planner is often insufficiently clear to indicate the means available and the circumstances in which they can be applied to solve a given problem. The more we become collectively committed, the more resources are available for allocation, the more significant the choice.

Given these ambiguities, then, it is understandable that there has been some confusion as to the meaning of the term "planning." Our inability to identify precisely these new problems, to comprehend theoretically the relevant variables, and to specify the identity and character of the planner, has made it difficult for us to conceptualize our problem-solving endeavors. No longer do we use qualifying phrases which connote the relevant variables with which the planner is concerned. More often we use phrases, such as "community planning," which tell us much more about where planning is being done than the nature of the problem to be solved. Similarly, the term "social planning" does little more than tell us that the problems under consideration are either societal or have to do with the social dimensions of one's life, or both—hardly a limiting conceptualization.

In our ignorance as to the relevant variables involved in the various problems with which we wish to cope, we slap these broad labels upon the recorded experience of particular attempts to solve problems, perhaps calling them "practice theory," and thereby intimate that (through the application of the label) we have found a general formula for planning, applicable to all social problems. It is common practice to set forth a formula such as the following:

1. Identify the problem.
2. Study and analyze it.
3. Bring together the relevant interests in the community.

4. Design a plan of action.
5. Implement the plan.
6. Evaluate the results.

This is a simplified schema, but it represents the essence of most practice theory. It fails to come to grips with the central issues of a planning effort. On what basis is the matter regarded as a problem? With respect to what is the problem to be studied? What determines the relevancy of interests? On what basis is choice made among alternative plans? What determines the feasibility of the plan? By what criteria are results to be evaluated? The answers to questions such as these are often provided or found by a planner in the course of a specific experience. These may be useful in the context of his immediate situation, but they cannot be generalized and cannot be used by other planners to understand the dimensions of their planning activities.

If we are to apply the planning method to the solution of complex mid-twentieth-century social problems—let alone apply it successfully—we must be able to identify the relationships among the relevant variables to the solutions of specific types of problems. In one sense, our ultimate aim would be to isolate (through identification and comprehension) the attempts of different types of persons to solve different types of problems—isolate them with such precision that our semantic references to these planning efforts would implicitly convey the relevant variables. There are current constructive trends of this kind in many fields of planning. In the area of economic planning we have come to identify a number of different types, including "gross national product planning," "deficit expenditure planning," and "growth" or "balanced economic planning." In city planning it is common to talk of "garden city planning," "regional planning," "central business district planning," and "new town planning." It is not the increasing use of such phrases that is important, but the fact that the usage of these terms reflects identification of recurring configurations of variables for different types of planning problems and, consequently, an increase in knowledgeable differentiation among problem-solving efforts that are deceptively similar in superficial appearance. Additional analysis may also reveal what variables, if any, are common to city, economic, mental health, and other forms of planning, despite their apparent dissimilarities.

The global term "social planning" encompasses at least three (and probably more) general types of efforts at social change. One kind seeks to alter human attitudes and behavioral patterns through education, exhortation, and a number of other methods for stimulating self-development and fulfillment. Within this category is an extensive variety of endeavors ranging from attempts to encourage board members of a social agency to assume roles of "civic leadership," to massive programs in community development, providing material resources and technical assistance to villages and regions of underdeveloped countries.

A second kind of social planning primarily strives to effect reforms in major legal and functional systems of a society. It relies upon political agitation, the application of research findings, legislation, litigation, administrative decisions, and a host of other instruments for coping with powerful trends and developments. It might include an attempt to eliminate a Jim Crow statute in Mississippi, as well as an attempt to enact legislation providing rent subsidies to individual citizens.

A third type of social planning, the one considered in this volume, tries to alter social conditions by changing the policies of formal organizations. It is undertaken in order to modify the amount, the quality, the accessibility, and the range of goods, services, and facilities provided for people. It includes efforts to persuade a senior citizens' organization to enrich its program of leisure-time activities, as well as struggles to revise procedures in a public welfare department.

Each of these general types of social planning has many subtypes. Moreover, the categories are somewhat arbitrary, for it is sometimes difficult to say that a particular planning experience fits one category but not another. For these reasons it is particularly important to achieve as narrow a focus as possible in analyzing planning; otherwise a systematic treatment is virtually impossible.

The third type is the one selected for discussion here. True, other types may have a greater long-run impact upon conditions of social welfare, but an overwhelming proportion of goods, services, and facilities in our society is provided through organizational activity. It is not too much to say that, in the aggregate, organizational policies will have a tremendous effect upon human welfare for a long time to come.

What follows is not a series of prescriptions for the "proper" methods of planning. Neither is it a set of propositions which, to date, have been documented by empirical evidence. It is an attempt to chart some of the major features that are a part of one common type of social planning, changing the policies of organizations. Our conviction that these features can be generalized does not in itself make them so. Their usefulness remains to be tested.

THE PLANNER

Our conceptual framework begins from the point of view of a single actor, that is, a discretely observable social entity engaged in an attempt to achieve a goal. Strictly speaking, there are many such entities or actors involved in the complex processes of change which we are trying to comprehend. They are all trying to achieve goals and solve problems. Their undertakings, in the aggregate, are often referred to as "community planning" or "community organization." [11] When this potpourri label is applied to the over-all process of a series of events, the qualification is usually made—quite soundly—that the interests, motives, and characteristics of these various individuals and organizations are quite different. We wish to comprehend as fully as possible the significance of the variance in interests, motives, and characteristics of the several actors in such complex planning processes. Yet, we will stay with one viewpoint and analyze situations at a level of generalization that, we hope, is applicable for other viewpoints as well.

Theoretically, our concern with the process of change as an interplay of multiple forces could be followed through from the point of view of each actor involved in a planning episode. Given sufficient empirical data, we could test our hypotheses as to the relationship between relevant variables from each of these points of view in turn. At this point, however, we will confine ourselves to the viewpoint of one actor so as not to complicate unduly an already complex task of comprehension. We will refer to him as a planner.

For the most part, planners are employed by organizations. Some of them function directly as staff to a single committee or organization created for a special project; others have many responsibilities within complex organizations. Some are employed by public agencies; others, by voluntary organizations. The common bond among all of them is that they undertake to change the policies of formal organizations in order to improve conditions of social welfare.

Realistically, it is difficult to distinguish planners from their

[11] "Community organization . . . is . . . a process by which a community identifies its needs or objectives, orders (or ranks) these needs or objectives, develops the confidence and will to work at these needs or objectives, finds the resources (internal and/or external) to deal with these needs or objectives, takes action in respect to them, and in so doing extends and develops cooperative and collaborative attitudes and practices in the community." Ross, *op. cit.*, p. 39.

employing organizations. In some measure, their interests, motivations, and means are those of their employers. Their decisions and actions are the products of a series of constraints—a mixture of personal, professional, and organizational considerations.[12]

Nonetheless, it is our conviction that, for several reasons, the elements of planning cannot be isolated, analyzed, or interpreted without first viewing the process from the perspective of the individual planner. One reason is that the present state of theory and knowledge as to the kinds of organizations that employ social planners is inadequate to provide a sound foundation for analysis from a corporate viewpoint. That individual planners are relatively comparable entities is rather evident, but it is not at all clear that the organizations employing them are sufficiently similar to be conceptually lumped together.

A second reason is that "organizational perceptions" depend upon the same cognitive facilities as a planner's. While organizational behavior is a product of complex interactions, it is carried out through individuals. Moreover, since one purpose of this book is to provide some useful generalizations to guide planning practice, it is worth noting that individuals can learn and organizations cannot. Naturally, the planner's position is different from that of all others within the organization, and he is subject to different constraints and incentives. But if the variables in planning can be isolated by using the perspective of one actor, they can, in turn, be reexamined from the other perspectives. Ultimately, one might combine these various individual perspectives with some understanding of the dynamics of interaction in various types of planning organizations.

A third reason is that most planners do have some freedom to decide and act. The interests, capacities, and commitments of the employing organization may play the major role in deter-

[12] See Braybrooke, "The Mystery of Executive Success Reexamined," *Administrative Science Quarterly*, VIII (1964), 533–60.

mining the course of a planning endeavor, but the individual planner usually has a chance to make some impact. In taking the viewpoint of the planner throughout this volume we shall distinguish, wherever pertinent, between those situations in which the planner has some latitude for decision and action and those in which he is severely constrained by his organizational setting.

THE PLANNER'S INFLUENCE

By "influence" we mean "the ability to get others to act, think, or feel as one intends." [13] This formulation by Banfield accurately reflects most of the definitions which have been set forth by social scientists.[14] It is only in their predictions and analyses as to who possesses sufficient influence to rule or govern large scopes, territories, or systems—such as entire communities—that scholars have differed as to the nature and locus of influence.[15]

[13] Banfield, *Political Influence*, p. 3.
[14] See, for example, de Jouvenel, *On Power*, and Dahl, "The Analysis of Influence in Local Communities," in Adrian, ed., *Social Science and Community Action*, pp. 25–42, hereafter cited as "Analysis of Influence."
[15] Essentially, these differences emanate from conflicting hypotheses as to the major renewable sources of influence in our society. Those generally referred to as "stratification theorists" have hypothesized that wealth and deference are not only the primary sources of renewable influence in American society, but also highly reliable indicators as to who rules or controls within a given community. Those generally referred to as "pluralists," on the other hand, hypothesize that a variety of factors—time, energy, formal authority, popularity, knowledge, ethnic identification, control over information—in addition to deference and wealth, can be quite significant sources of influence. They suggest that important sources of influence are multiple, shifting in importance in accordance with the given ends which an actor desires to achieve. The pluralists maintain, then, that while wealth and deference may be reliable indices of influence in certain specified situations, they are not often likely to be reliable indices of sufficient influence to rule or govern.
    For the most part, these differing views have been reflected in methodological debates. Both social stratificationists and pluralists have conducted studies to test their hypotheses. The stratificationists have been criticized because their methodology has virtually assured validation of their hypotheses before the fact. For a succinct statement of these criticisms, see Bachrach and Baratz, "Two Faces of Power," *American Political Science Review*, LVI (1962),

It is not necessary for us to take sides in this debate. Social planners do not possess sufficient influence to govern or to carry out utopian schemes.[16] Yet they have adequate influence for achieving certain ends. Many things can be said about a planner's use of influence without the need to consider the distribution and nature of influence in a total community or system. While planners may not play essential roles in governing communities (although in some instances they may), their efforts currently involve thousands of people and millions of dollars. We wish to understand these efforts.

CHANGES IN CONDITIONS
OF SOCIAL WELFARE

To suggest that a planner is trying to change conditions of social welfare is not to move very far in precisely defining the nature of social planning. In the strictest sense, a concern with social welfare can be said to be as broad as total concern for all aspects of collective life. No teacher or practitioner of social welfare would claim that his interests, as a citizen, were any less than those identified by Jeremy Bentham as the ends of the state—subsistence, abundance, security, equality (general wellbeing)—the greatest good for the greatest number.[17]

947–52. For an exhaustive critical examination of eight major social stratification studies, see Polsby, *Community Power and Political Theory.*

The pluralists have been criticized on two counts. One criticism has been concerned with the difficulties of using pluralist methodology—difficulties in gaining access to the kinds of information required by the methodology as well as difficulties engendered by the extensive investment of time, manpower, and financial resources required to execute the methodology. (See *ibid.* for a brief outline of the research approach necessary to test the pluralists' hypotheses as to the nature and locus of power in a community.) Pluralists have also been criticized for focusing upon issues which have not embodied matters of ultimate importance to the community. Bachrach and Baratz (*op. cit.*) maintain that matters of true importance to the community are suppressed by the holders of wealth and deference—never allowed to become issues in the community.

[16] See Meyerson, "The Utopian Tradition and the Planning of Cities," *Dædalus*, XC (1961), 180–93.

[17] See Halévy, *The Growth of Philosophic Radicalism*, pp. 45–52.

The notion of social welfare which we shall employ in this volume is somewhat narrower, and is essentially defined in practice by the social work profession. Some social workers would hold (with persuasiveness) that they are professionally attuned to the broad ultimate goals set forth above. But most would agree that their direct social welfare concerns can be identified by two measures.

One boundary of social welfare as a profession can be found in those aspects of the human condition which public and private organizations try to meet through direct and immediate preventive or treatment measures.[18] While national economic and defense programs are designed to have an ultimate, indirect impact in meeting some of the same needs as those served by social welfare programs, a definitive characteristic of the latter is immediate and direct contact with the persons in need. Such a definition at least includes attention to housing, employment, income maintenance, medical care, retirement, education, recreation, and legal aid. In advanced industrial societies, elaborate organizational superstructures have come to play an important role in administering and coordinating these kinds of programs. Nonetheless, the focus of efforts is still on the individual, even if he is found at the end of a long administrative pipeline. While, for example, the administrative and operational framework of the social security system is quite impersonal, it ultimately establishes personal contact, directly

[18] Since the evolution of a social concern with human relationships emerged from family, religious, and charitable preoccupations, it is customary to identify the social dimension by its individual expression—the need of each distinctive human being. The extent of aggregate social concern, reflected in collective policies and measures, is frequently overlooked. In 1960, some $40 billion of local, state, federal, and philanthropic funds was expended for social welfare purposes. (*Encyclopedia of Social Work*, Table 17, p. 874.) This includes expenditures for social insurances, including old age and survivors insurance, retirement of public employees, unemployment insurance, and temporary disability, as well as the more conventional public assistance employment service and health and welfare medical programs of the various jurisdictions. Over sixty million persons of all ages in the United States are directly affected by a single federal program, compulsory old age and survivors insurance.

providing for specific individuals (albeit with the aid of computers).

A second characteristic of social welfare is attention directed to particular, identifiable subgroups in society. While social welfare is sometimes concerned with the indirect impact of programs upon general societal conditions, the anticipated result is usually seen in relation to more easily identified groups in society—"the elderly"; "the indigent"; "actual or potential delinquents"; "the mentally retarded"—reflecting a view that one set of needs has priority over others. While government strives to enhance "the general welfare" of its jurisdiction, social welfare tries to enhance the particular welfares of many persons or of a particular kind of person.

"IMPROVEMENTS" IN SOCIAL WELFARE

Our conception of an "improvement" in conditions of social welfare is not tied to an ethical theory. In the context of our analysis any initial goal selected by a planner because he feels it is meritorious will be treated for purposes of discussion as a potential improvement. We will attempt to comprehend his struggles to achieve it, or to attain as much of it as he can. If he achieves his goal even partially, he can be regarded as having achieved an improvement.

Our conceptual assumption that the planner's goal—any goal—is an improvement does not, however, completely confine us to a realm of pure moral relativism. Since social welfare activities are defined as attempts to meet needs of specified individuals or subgroups, some indices can be applied *after the fact* to determine if needs have actually been met. If they have, then an improvement has taken place. This retrospective evaluation, of course, is not of much aid to the planner who would like to have a reliable index to use in selecting the most effective approach for coping with a social problem. Clearly, a measure that has been documented as effective in meeting a given type of human need will be preferred by a social planner. But until we have accumulated far more hard evidence as to the effects of various programs, procedures, and provisions—until it is established that some approaches meet certain needs better than others—planners will have to exercise some value preference in selecting steps for improving social welfare.

CHANGING POLICIES OF FORMAL ORGANIZATIONS

Efforts to improve conditions of social welfare can range from attempts to change the behavior of individuals to changing the broadest social conditions (see Chapter IV). Any force or variable which man can harness for his own ends can be a tool for social planning. In fact, virtually every goal pursued by any social planner can be viewed as a means to achieving a broader goal. By the same token, any means for implementing a goal can be seen as a goal in itself, with alternative means, in turn, relevant to its achievement. An endless circle of semantics can develop as we struggle with this chain of ends and means in attempting to conceptualize.

One way to deal with the problem is to use terms which reflect the content of goals and subgoals or means and submeans as we try to characterize the linkage between them. Thus, for example, it is possible to develop a series of distinctions, such as "preamble goals," "policy goals," and "planning goals." "Preamble goal" would be the term applied to the end which most people in the planner's society would accept as normative, a culturally self-evident goal: "improving the lives of the elderly." A policy goal developed from this preamble goal might be "the development of better housing for the elderly of San Francisco." A planning goal might be "the construction of 5,000 new public housing units for the elderly in San Francisco, within the next 36 months."

The use of these and other labels is convenient for purposes of discussion in dealing with this chain. In considering a single planning problem the specification of labels can be agreed upon, and it then becomes possible to proceed with discussion. The labels have a limited conceptual usefulness, however, in that in any given planning problem a persuasive argument could be made for placing these labels at any of several segments in the goal-goal-means-means chain.

Our approach will be to cut into this chain at the point where the planner is attempting to change the policy of a formal organization in order to improve conditions of social welfare for the elderly. When his efforts reflect this aim, we shall call it his goal.

How does an organization come to be selected as a target of planned change, and how does it differ from other targets often chosen in social planning? Many types of targets can be identified. A very general one is the citizenry of a community; a more specific target might be those citizens who may have some influence over community decisions. An entirely different type of target consists of formally constituted organizations, such as social agencies, government authorities, churches, and professional societies. The capacity of these organizations to allocate resources that affect conditions of social welfare often brings them to the planner's attention. As a result, planning for social change is frequently directed at organizational policies.

In analyzing this type of planning our primary concern will be the feasibility of goals which are at the same time proposals for an innovation in the allocation of an organization's resources. We will not give major attention to strategies for implementing feasible goals or to the question of whether a certain goal represents the "correct" solution to a given social problem. These are important matters, but not central to the present analysis. Much of the discussion may indicate steps through which a planner can increase the effectiveness of his strategies and the "correctness" of his solutions. The main object, however, will be to consider the factors that determine when and why any goal is feasible, that is, possible to achieve. An understanding of these factors provides an effective basis for a choice among alternative goals and courses of implementing action.

II · THE ANATOMY OF FEASIBILITY

Although we have singled out for analysis one type of social planning endeavor, we have hardly begun to consider the relationships among the variables that determine the feasibility of planning. It may be useful to lay them out in brief, outline form, before proceeding in greater detail.

The range of variables subject to our scrutiny will be relatively confined. While the decisions and actions of planners can be seen within the context of an endless chain of relationships and phenomena, primary attention will be devoted to the immediate variables found in the direct relationship between the planner, his goals, and the organization whose policy he is trying to change. However, some attention will have to be given to additional factors. Behind the planner stands the organization which he represents. Planners are employed under varying circumstances for different reasons, and carry diverse responsibilities. In addition, planners are subject to a variety of personal and professional constraints as well as to organizational considerations.

Similarly, the organization in which a policy change is desired must be viewed against an extensive backdrop. Organizations, as all collectivities, can only be understood in terms of the individuals and groups—with conflicting aims, motives, and needs—that comprise them. Especially when one views organizations that are not essentially profit-making organizations—and those with which we are concerned, for the most part, are not—it is extremely difficult to identify their corpo-

rate goals. In contemporary society, this is even tending to become difficult in the case of profit-making organizations; for
businesses are becoming increasingly aware of their corporate
image and desire to identify themselves as champions of "the
public interest." Mixtures of profit-making aims, concern for
the corporate image, and the private motives of individuals
who comprise organizations render corporate goals extremely
ambiguous.

It is also necessary to keep in mind all the persons, organizations, informal groups, and strategies involved in planning, and
even the ultimate ramifications of various policy changes
which might be made by an organization. No analysis of an attempt to solve a social problem can ignore these factors. The
interests of society at large, competing organizations, and other
planners and actors are but some of the important variables in
the planning process.

In delineating a relatively narrow and direct range for our
discussion, then, we are not wholly excluding these matters.
We will consider them as they are seen by the planner when he
is attempting to achieve his goal.

THE DEVELOPMENT OF GOALS

The selection of a goal as a solution for a given social welfare problem is not necessarily undertaken wholly by the
planner. In some cases his employing organization may present
him with the assignment of achieving a goal that has already
been firmly determined. In others, a goal may be developed
through the joint efforts of the planner and a committee he
staffs, as they review data and explore various possibilities. On
some occasions the planner is relatively free to develop and
select the planning goal.

Social planning goals, as suggested in Chapter I, contain
measures for meeting human needs. Yet, given a concern for

meeting need, there are many possible approaches to doing so. Which one or ones are selected will depend upon a number of factors including, for example, an interpretation or diagnosis of the genesis or cause of the need. At present, in most areas of social welfare, the efficacy of one approach to meeting needs, as opposed to another, is not clearly established.

Regardless of the combination of parties participating in the development of a goal, it consists of interpretations as to effective solutions of a social problem, preferred because they are identified as having merit.[1] This goal—which might be called the "preference goal"—reflects the first series of choices on the long path of planning.

It goes without saying that the preference goal is not the planner's ideal, ultimately perfect solution to the problem under consideration. He is not omnipotent. What he can accomplish is limited by his capacity for wielding influence. It is also clear that the goal is formulated with a recognition that the planner possesses *some* influence, since it is assumed that he will be able to effect some change. A preference goal, then, is neither a utopian scheme nor an affirmation of the *status quo*. It is a goal which embodies some estimate of feasibility, for the assumption is almost always made, even if implicitly, that it can be achieved.[2] At the same time, it is not necessarily a feasible goal; it is particularly unlikely to be so if an analysis of feasibility is not explicit and relatively thorough. But this analysis is extremely difficult to perform completely and competently because each preference goal is characterized by its own situation of feasibility.

[1] As Wilson has suggested, a defining characteristic of planning is "the selection of ends . . . 'on their merits.'" See "An Overview of Theories of Planned Change," in Morris, ed., *Centrally Planned Change,* p. 13.

[2] See Braybrooke and Lindblom, *A Strategy of Decision.*

The components comprising the feasibility of any planning goal vary according to the nature and extent of influence possessed by the planner and the nature of the problem to be solved. The relationship between these determines the feasibility of each planning endeavor. The problem to be solved in the kind of planning discussed here is the overcoming of an organization's resistance to the policy change presented in a preference goal. To estimate feasibility a planner must have a fairly accurate picture of the character and extent of the resistance which an organization will offer to a given policy change and its relationship to the influence that he possesses. It should be noted, however, that the relationship is not primarily quantitative. The *kind* of influence and the *kind* of resistance are components of feasibility as well. Some kinds of influence are useful for overcoming some kinds of resistance, but not others. Whether or not the two match will importantly shape later features of a planning endeavor.

The planner has much to gain by an accurate assessment of feasibility. While it may not enable him to predict accurately the precise course of planning, it can clarify alternatives available for achieving maximum results from his investment of planning resources. If, for purposes of simplification, we momentarily eliminate *kinds* of influence and *kinds* of resistance from our consideration, it may be possible to visualize the alternative possibilities.

An accurate estimate of major organizational resistance will forewarn a planner of a difficult path ahead. If, in fact, he has influence sufficient to overcome this major resistance, his correct assessment will prepare him for an extensive expenditure of his resources and for the likely ramifications of doing so. On the other hand, if his influence is clearly insufficient, his accurate assessment will protect him from fruitlessly expending his resources. Moreover, his attention will be redirected from a preference goal that will not lead to the accomplishment of a change to a consideration of other approaches. An accurate estimate of the situation is also helpful if both organizational resistance and resources for planning influence are minor; the planner can avoid an excessive use of resources in accomplishing an essentially simple task.

Similarly, a failure to comprehend the situation can be quite costly. If the planner does not perceive that organizational resistance will be minor and that, consequently, little influence will be needed, he may use up many valuable resources for no reason. Or, if his influence is minor and he does not anticipate major organizational resistance, he will waste resources in a hopeless cause.

If we were to add to this picture an analysis of the kinds and character of resistance and the kinds and character of influence, the difficulty as well as the significance of an accurate assessment would become even more apparent. Despite all the difficulties, however, a more thorough estimate of feasibility than is usually undertaken can greatly reduce costs of, and increase opportunities for, achievement.

The planner can try to assess organizational resistance from one of two perspectives, depending on whether he assesses before or after he actually encounters resistance. If he attempts the assessment before encountering resistance, he is trying to *predict* the organization's behavior. If he assesses after he encounters resistance, he is trying to *analyze* the organization's behavior. In both cases, however, he is concerned with the same set of variables. These variables are the elements involved in that particular organization's policy development. In other words, he is concerned with answering the general question: "How is policy determined in that organization?"

The target organization is only one side of the picture. A planner is naturally concerned with his supply of tools for changing policy. He can list his resources, but many on the list may have no usefulness for the purpose at hand. Will they provide him with influence for overcoming the resistance of the organization in question? It is often difficult for a planner to know until he has tried them out, perhaps wasting many if not all of them. Whether resources are effective for overcoming the resistance of an organization is largely determined by the primary interests of those groups that dominate its policy. Which planning proposals grossly violate their major interests to such a degree that they cannot be influenced at all? If the degree of change sought by the planner is relatively tolerable, yet resisted by the organization, to what kinds of influence will the policy group be responsive? Not only must a planner comprehend all this in order to identify the resources which will be useful, but also he needs to know which of his many apparent resources can actually be mobilized.

If the planner is to enhance his effectiveness and reduce waste of planning resources, he must be able to understand simultaneously the relationships among all these factors. These relationships represent the feasibility of his goal and his entire undertaking. Comprehension of them distinguishes the possible from the impossible and the more possible from the less possible. It provides a glimpse at the likely consequences of today's plans and activities, and a guide to immediate decisions and steps. To gain the advantages of understanding feasibility, a planner must bring together the full set of pertinent factors —preference goal, target organization, policy faction, resources, and responses to differential influences.

Preserving the Merit in Preference Goals

A planner confronted by an unfeasible situation does not have to give up his planning effort. In many cases unfeasibility is due to a mismatch between the kinds of influence to which a policy faction is responsive and the resources for influence possessed by the planner. A planner can do a number of things to bring about a match between the two, making it possible to achieve his preference goal. As we will see when we consider these opportunities, a knowledgeable approach to unfeasible situations can increase a planner's ability to overcome obstacles. A planner with inadequate influence need not relinquish his utopian ideals by capitulating to resistance. To be guided by feasibility is not to accommodate to superior force, but to anticipate the best available means for achieving the desirable.

III · EXPERIENCES IN SOCIAL PLANNING

In the theoretical discussions comprising the chapters that follow, frequent reference will be made, for purposes of illustration, to recent planning experiences. This illustrative material is drawn from three-year demonstration projects in planning for the elderly, conducted in four American communities: San Francisco; Contra Costa County, California; Denver; and Worcester, Massachusetts. The projects were financed primarily by grants from the Ford Foundation to local planning organizations.[1] These grants enabled each sponsoring agency to employ a full-time staff member (a project director), who was expected to make use of existing community resources in an effort to develop and expand programs and services for the elderly. The sponsoring agencies, typical health and welfare organizations located in metropolitan areas, were free to pursue this broad purpose as they saw fit.

Brief descriptions of some of the planning undertaken in each of these projects are presented in this chapter simply to provide background for ensuing discussion. The descriptions, necessarily, are highly selective and cannot reproduce the

[1] The four projects were part of a larger program, which included three other projects. (The three that will not be discussed here were conducted by the committee on aging of the Health and Welfare Council of Metropolitan St. Louis, the governor's commission on aging in Minnesota, and the Golden Years, Inc., of Marion County, Kans.) Altogether, the Ford Foundation appropriated about $320,000 for the demonstration projects. Roughly two thirds of this sum were distributed among the seven sponsoring organizations. The remainder was awarded to the Florence Heller Graduate School for Advanced Studies in Social Welfare, Brandeis University, for research and coordination of the projects.

flavor and richness of the actual experiences. Nonetheless, objectives, decisions, obstacles, activities, results, and other elements contained in these episodes can serve as a foundation for
later considerations of planning feasibility. Analysis of this material will be presented in following chapters.

THE DEMONSTRATION PROJECTS

The Ford grant program in planning for the aging was one
expression of the Foundation's general attempt to direct the attention of American institutions to pressing social problems
and, especially, to fresh approaches to their solution. Changes
in American society have engendered social and psychological
conditions which have introduced unfamiliar strains in the
lives of older persons. Health and welfare programs, unaccus-
tomed to dealing with these conditions, have been unable
to cope with them effectively. Attempts to deal with these
changes have been undertaken throughout the country as well
as in the communities selected for special projects by the
Foundation.

The welfare of the elderly has become a fresh problem in
Western society because of the convergence of two major
trends: an explosive increase in the number of those who live
beyond the age of 65 and the rapid advance of industrial technology.[2] Since 1900 the percentage of persons over 65 in the
United States has grown at a rate three times the percentage
increase of the total population. In 1965 nearly nineteen million persons were past 65; one third of them were over 75, and
15,000 of them were more than 100 years of age. The number of
older persons suffering from physical, economic, and social
handicaps today was not dreamed of a generation ago. At the
same time, advanced technology has made older workers rela-

[2] Numerous reports deal with these trends and are sources for the data.
See especially Tibbits, ed., *Handbook of Social Gerontology;* and *The Nation and
Its Older People: Report of the White House Conference on Aging.*

tively dispensable as a source of productive labor. Changes in educational and occupational patterns, and developments in transportation and communication systems, have affected the nature of family ties as adult children have been increasingly inclined to make their homes in cities distant from their parents.

These trends have produced certain crises in the role, status, and maintenance of older persons. As it has become commonplace for persons over sixty-five to anticipate an average of ten, fifteen, and even twenty years after retirement, the anomalous social position and identity of unemployed persons has emerged as an increasingly important issue. Moreover, on the average, income drops by at least one half after retirement. This reduction in income makes it difficult if not impossible for a third to one half of all older persons to have adequate nutrition, clothing, recreation, and medical care.

Although many older persons continue in relatively good health throughout a substantial proportion of their retirement years, health remains a source of anxiety. Chronic illness, with its far-reaching consequences, is a constant threat. Seventy-five percent of all persons over sixty-five suffer from a disabling illness or condition.[3] Older persons require hospitalization four times as often as does the typical American. They often need special kinds of medical care and supervision: not dramatic treatment, for subsequent recovery and discharge of the patient, but medical surveillance over long periods of time, as minor changes in their condition take place. This type of care makes especially heavy demands upon the time of medical personnel and also requires far more complementary, nonmedical services than are provided through present programs.

The changing needs and strains for older persons are reflected in numerous ways. There is a definite, though not delib-

[3] National Health Survey, *Duration of Limitations of Activity Due to Chronic Conditions, United States, July 1959—June 1960.*

erate, trend toward institutionalizing older persons. Since 1945 proprietary nursing homes, with as many beds as there are in hospitals throughout the country, have become a major institutional resource. Mental hospitals have become collecting points for confused and enfeebled older persons; the proportion of the elderly who live in mental hospitals is extraordinarily high, especially because younger patients are discharged with greater frequency. The elderly constitute as much as 30 percent of the patients in many hospitals for acute diseases.

Another expression of these trends is the growing isolation of large numbers of older persons. Many live clustered together in low-rent accommodations in the center of large cities. Other elderly people, with higher incomes, are segregated in special new towns for the elderly built under commercial auspices. Many older persons face uncertainty in their family relationships because more and more families consist of three and sometimes four or five generations scattered throughout the country. There is little precedent to guide families as to their appropriate responsibility for the oldest generation, especially when the total family income is limited.[4]

These emergent needs of the elderly have been a subject of greater national attention since 1961 when the President of the United States convened a White House Conference on Aging. For some years the federal government and private organizations, such as the Ford Foundation and the National Council on the Aging, have administered programs designed to discover ways of dealing with the problems confronting older persons. While the national programs have made funds and guidelines available, the responsibility for development of facilities and service programs has rested largely with local organizations. The Ford Foundation projects in San Francisco, Contra Costa, Denver, and Worcester were undertaken to stimulate such organizations to carry out this responsibility. Per-

[4] See Schorr, *Filial Responsibility in the Modern American Family.*

haps because of the implied expectations of the Foundation itself, each applicant for a grant proposed: (1) to mobilize local resources; (2) to demonstrate that local community organization constitutes an effective approach to planning for the elderly; (3) to arouse general citizen interest in the needs of older persons; (4) to extend existing agency services rather than to stimulate or create new and additional services.

While each of the projects was sponsored by a health and welfare council, and the major conditions affecting the elderly were substantially the same in the four communities, some variations among the settings are worth noting.[5] There were considerable differences in the populations of the areas encompassed by the planning projects. At one extreme is Worcester, the industrial and commercial center of a metropolitan area about forty miles west of Boston, with a population of 323,000. At the other is San Francisco, the core city of a metropolitan area of nearly 3,000,000 persons. Contra Costa County has approximately 400,000, and the four counties within the scope of the Denver project total about a half million.

Contra Costa, across the bay from San Francisco, was primarily a rural area a little more than a generation ago. During the Second World War, however, several small towns in the western part of the county became major shipbuilding and oil-refining centers, attracting considerable industrial manpower. Since the war, Contra Costa has also been a suburban retreat for many persons employed in San Francisco and nearby cities. Between 1940 and 1960, while both the state of California and other Bay counties increased in population by 200 percent, Contra Costa increased by 400 percent. In 1960, Contra Costa was acquiring new residents at the rate of 2,000 per month. At

---

[5] Data on the populations and the economic conditions in the four communities are taken from the *U.S. Census, 1950* and *1960.* Data on United Fund contributions were supplied by the United Community Funds and Councils of America.

present, more than half of the people in the county live in a few, heavily industrialized, densely populated towns.

The other project communities, of course, were not experiencing such marked social and economic change. Each had been a well-developed urban center for many years, with relatively stable populations and economic bases. Denver and San Francisco are still growing and will continue to do so for many years, but the steady, continued growth of these communities is not likely to have major effects upon their fundamental characters. While Worcester lost some of its industry during the 1950s, its economy is still healthy and its population stable.

A comparison of the percentages of older persons in the four communities provides some indication of the extent to which the growth of the Far Western communities, particularly Contra Costa, is attributable to recent migrations of younger persons from other parts of the nation. In the Worcester area, 13.6 percent of the population is sixty-five years and older. The percentages of older persons in San Francisco and Contra Costa are 8.4 and 5.5, respectively. (The Contra Costa proportion is expected to triple within a decade.) Persons sixty-five and over comprise 12 percent of the population in Denver. These proportions compare with a national average of about 10 percent.

Median family income is substantially higher in Contra Costa ($7,327) and San Francisco ($7,092) than in Denver ($6,551) and Worcester ($6,058). Yet, in 1963, Worcester's United Fund raised far more per capita ($6.44) than did the Funds in the other communities. The Denver Fund raised $4.43. Contributions from San Francisco and Contra Costa were combined in a single Bay area campaign that yielded $3.86 (slightly below the national average of $3.95 per capita); when these contributions were allocated to the various social agencies in the Bay area, San Francisco received about four times as much as Contra Costa.

San Francisco

San Francisco has a great number and variety of voluntary social welfare organizations, whose boards and committees are dominated by members of wealthy, old-line families. These civic leaders take great pride in the programs and services provided by their agencies, but are relatively conservative in adapting their policies to meet changing conditions such as those currently affecting the elderly. San Francisco has a Mayor's Commission on Aging, but most activity in this field has been undertaken by the Social Planning Department of the United Community Fund, which was given the Ford grant.

Nearly all of the voluntary and most of the public agencies in San Francisco have at least a nominal relationship with the Fund or its planning department. While the Social Planning Department has a certain degree of autonomy in the selection of matters for study and in the development of policy recommendations, its primary function is to support or oppose financial applications submitted by social agencies to the United Fund. The Fund maintains strict control over all efforts to raise philanthropic funds. The Fund and the planning department are enmeshed in a complex regional mechanism known as the United Bay Area Crusade, which purports to guide and direct the voluntary fund-raising in five counties, including San Francisco. The Crusade is advised on planning matters by the Bay Area Welfare Planning Federation, which has only one full-time professional employee.

The Social Planning Department maintains four district councils which serve different ethnic areas of the city; three continuing service councils for group work, health, family and children's care; and three special project committees on youth, urban development, and the aging (established specifically to manage the Ford demonstration project).

Concern with the needs of the elderly in San Francisco dates from at least 1942 when a study of family and child welfare services stressed the need to extend casework services to the elderly. In 1953, the Chronic Illness Service Center, one of the first in the United States, made a series of recommendations to enlarge services for the chronically ill elderly. In 1956, the United Community Fund organized an *ad hoc* committee on the aging which, after a lengthy study, recommended a permanent council on aging with full-time professional staff. No funds were allocated for this purpose, however, and responsibility for planning for the elderly remained dispersed among the various specialized councils for family and child welfare, group work and recreation, and health. In 1959, the volunteer chairmen of the several subcommittees on aging in the various councils of the Fund jointly appealed for an over-all committee on aging with staff. It was this interest which led to the sponsorship of the Ford project, the San Francisco Program for the Aging (SPA).

The SPA had the full-time staff services of one social worker and a secretary. Professional staff of the Fund's various councils were presumably available for technical assistance as needed. The project was conducted in the traditional style of social planning in San Francisco, with heavy reliance upon volunteer committees. The SPA generated more than twenty-five special committees during the course of the Ford demonstration. These included an executive committee; a steering committee, which met infrequently; an advisory panel, which was never convened; four operating committees (health, medical care, and rehabilitation; casework; education, recreation, and group services; housing, employment, preretirement preparation, and income maintenance). Out of each of these, in turn, came a variety of subcommittees. For example, the committee concerned with casework services appointed four major subcommittees on goals, casework services, friendly visiting, and professional training, which frequently broke down into sub-subcommittees to carry forward each task.

Over-all, the committees and subcommittees totaled 240 persons, including directors of social agencies, wealthy and respected members of old-line families, educators, leading churchmen, directors of municipal departments, physicians and attorneys.[6] While this elaboration of committees served to engage the loyal attention of many able individuals, it also complicated planning activities to a considerable extent. For example, one of the project's proposals, involving an expenditure of only $40,000 over a two-year period, was subjected to the scrutiny of ten separate committees—six committees of the SPA and four committees of the American Red Cross, the agency which would administer the service in question. And the proposal was still subject to review by the board of the United Fund even though the money was to be provided by some source other than the Fund.

The San Francisco application for a Ford grant set these general goals:

1. Improvement of public and private programs
2. Arousal of interest in the community to move it into action for improved services for the aged
3. Creation of machinery for coordinating services for the elderly

More specific goals emerged in the course of the project. While these seem to follow a logical course of systematic development, in fact, they developed erratically, in response to various pressures, interests, and events:

A. Casework and Personal Counseling Services
    1. Additional caseworkers to be employed or reassigned for work with the elderly, especially by the department of public welfare, but also by hospitals, the Family Service Association, and the Jewish Family Service

[6] See Kravitz, "Sources of Leadership Input for Social Welfare Planning."

2. The department of welfare to organize a special training program for its staff; a school of social work to organize a training program on the needs of the aged for all agency staffs

3. Discontinuance of joint case services provided by the voluntary family agencies to public assistance recipients, in order to encourage staff increases within the department of welfare

4. The public welfare department to expend all funds annually appropriated to it through an increase in allocation for professional services to clients

5. The local chapter of the American Red Cross to sponsor a program of friendly visiting to supplement professional casework services, to be financed by a local foundation

B. Health, Medical Care, and Rehabilitation
1. Initiate a system of health examinations and referrals for the elderly without family physicians
   a) To be located in several public health centers
   b) To be administered by the local medical society
   c) To be financed from a grant by the Public Health Service
2. Persuade the city health department to increase all of its public health services and to include auxiliary services, such as homemaking and home nursing for the aged
3. Support adequate payment for public assistance recipients in nursing homes

C. Adult Education and Recreation
1. Bring leisure-time services within reach of residents in all parts of the city by:
   a) Inducing agencies operating leisure-time programs under sectarian auspices to extend their services to all near-by residents
   b) Increasing the scope of responsibility of the nonsectarian senior citizens' center
   c) Reallocating service-area responsibilities among all existing agencies
2. Launch a training program about leisure-time needs of the aging, conducted by a school of social work and directed both to sectarian and to nonsectarian agencies
3. Persuade the municipal recreation department to begin a program of in-service training for its own staff
4. Influence the municipal library to adopt more favorable

policies in handling indigent older persons who use its facilities

5. Induce the Canon Kip Community House to organize a special center for the socially isolated aged

6. Arrange for agencies working in the North Market area to
cooperate in case referrals and to establish better liaison
with the Hotel Association whose constituent members in
this area house a large number of older persons

D. Retirement Policies

1. Encourage the state employment service to assign special
vocational counselors to advise older unemployed persons
and to help them locate employment

2. Organize, with the cooperation of the California department
of employment and the U.S. Office of Manpower, Automation,
and Training, a special retraining program for older unemployed workers

3. Stimulate adult education organizations to offer classes in
retirement preparation

E. Housing

1. Persuade the redevelopment authority to arrange for the
construction of 800 units to house older persons soon to be
displaced by downtown urban renewal projects

2. Persuade the housing authority to incorporate social services
and facilities in its low-cost public housing projects

3. Organize a housing information service

The emergence of so many planning goals in the San Francisco project can be attributed, in large measure, to the Social
Planning Department's established practice of creating a separate subcommittee to deal with almost every matter. Each of
the various committees, subcommittees, and sub-subcommittees
of the SPA evolved its own set of planning objectives.

Recreation.—As the Ford project began, the SPA formed a
special committee of representatives from several senior citizens' centers and recreation groups serving the aged, which
were primarily interested in providing limited recreational programs for their own members and in building up their respective memberships. The SPA sought to enrich these organiza-

tions' approach to group work with the elderly and to introduce a more varied program of creative leisure-time activity.
To this end, the project director provided extensive information and educational materials. Census data concerning the
characteristics and residential situations of the aged were analyzed and presented to indicate the concentration of lonely
older persons in downtown San Francisco, a section not served
by any of the many senior centers established throughout the
city. Evidence as to poor service coverage was brought to light.
Some forty senior citizens' centers were operating, sponsored
by the Catholic Committee for the Aging, the Council of
Churches, the Jewish Community Center, the city's recreation
department, and a variety of settlement houses and other nonsectarian agencies. However, less than 3 percent of the elderly
population came into contact with these programs, and only
half of these attended with any regularity. On the basis of
these data, the SPA proposed expansion in the volume, clientele, and service areas of existent programs.

This proposal met a negative response from the agency representatives on SPA's recreation committee. Each of the sponsoring organizations emphasized the importance of its distinctive religious and cultural appeal, although each was, of
course, "open to participation by anyone who wished to come."
The SPA's documentation of disparities between the location
and character of potential clients and the location and character of existent programs was countered with the remark that
"people prefer to travel to centers of their own choice rather
than being limited to one in their immediate neighborhood."
Evidence indicating that centers were currently used only by
persons who were living in the immediate neighborhoods had
little effect.

The planner then used population data to support a plan for
organizing a series of district and neighborhood centers sponsored by existing institutions, but this proposal was considered

too ambitious and was tabled. The planner also tried to enrich conceptions of group work with the aging by bringing in several consultants to address the recreation committee and by encouraging enrollment in special courses offered at the University of California. But the only result of nearly three years of effort was a statement on behalf of the committee indicating that the diversity of existing recreation programs was well recognized and, moreover, justified because "diversity is essential for providing the older person with a choice." The gross lack of coverage was not mentioned in the final report.

Failing to alter the program pattern of the recreation agencies, the project director next directed attention to older persons living downtown, where services and facilities were virtually nonexistent. Through interviews with agency staffs and with older persons, the planner developed a full picture of the lonely life led by the elderly of the area, and established quite clearly that few conformed to the stereotype of "derelict," "wino," "failure of society." Nevertheless, efforts to persuade a community center to establish a program or assume some responsibility for these people were unsuccessful. After two years of continuous expressions of "interest," the director of this center could only say that his board had "not yet" taken any steps to seek the necessary funds.

The chairman of the recreation subcommittee was sufficiently disturbed by the failure to launch a nonsectarian city program that she turned to her own church in the hope of making some progress. Her activities led to the establishment of a downtown Catholic senior center. While this result may be considered a by-product of the planner's work, neither the planner nor the SPA capitalized on the subcommittee chairman's associations and influence in the Catholic community. Initiative was taken by the chairman herself, without committee action or support.

The planner gave attention to recreational needs in another

section of the city, the North Market area, where a large number of older persons live alone in cheap hotels and rooming houses. Since this area was served by a variety of public health and casework agencies, plus the Salvation Army and the YWCA, representatives of each were brought together as a special committee under the leadership of a prominent lay spokesman for the Protestant Council of Churches. The planner, however, saw this committee primarily as an interagency case conference which could lay the foundation for coordinated effort in the district. To this end, the chief of the community mental health service was brought in to meet with the committee monthly, and the activities and problems of each agency staff member were reported. In effect, the North Market committee provided a forum where social workers exchanged information about their casework experiences, but it threw no light on the general problem of coping with the situation in the North Market area. Even when the San Francisco Hotel Association requested the establishment of a central and authoritative information source to which its members could turn for help with the welfare problems of their residents, the committee did not respond.

Health.—Most of the efforts of the SPA to meet health needs of the elderly were concentrated in an attempt to establish a health screening service which would embody principles of education, prevention, and rehabilitation, and stimulate interagency cooperation and coordination. Responsibility for developing this program was transferred from the project director to the health services consultant of the Social Planning Department, who acted as a planner in succeeding periods. A subcommittee was established consistent with the San Francisco pattern of relying on volunteer committees of influential individuals. The chairman was the director of a geriatric project at the Langley Porter clinic, an internationally famous psychiatric institution. The planner procured evidence from senior citizens' centers as to the health problems of their clientele. These data uniformly indicated that most of the center participants did not have family doctors (having frequently outlived their former physicians) and that there was an evident lack of continuity in physician-patient relationships at various public clinics. The health screening proposal evolved in an attempt to overcome these inadequacies.

As soon as the general outlines of the proposal began to take shape, the planning staff established liaison with social agencies that were in a position either to provide services or to refer patients to the screening team. Simultaneously, they began to inform various professional organizations about the proposal. The city health department, which had been involved since the early stages of this effort, was asked to make space available for the screening service in its five district health offices. It only agreed to provide space in one or, possibly, two district units. The San Francisco medical society was officially approached for participation and cooperation, with the proposal that the screening be done for diagnostic purposes with referrals for treatment made to private physicians only. This promised liaison with the medical society enhanced the health department's enthusiasm for the screening proposal. Several agencies (including the public health department, the public welfare department, and the Visiting Nurse Association) were asked to administer the program, but the medical society was the prime choice for sponsorship. It approved the project in principle and appointed five members to work out the details, with an obstetrician assuming the chairmanship of the project committee. The chairman and the other members of the medical society who eventually dominated committee activity proved to be unrelentingly opposed to the original health proposal, fearing that it would detract from the accustomed responsibility of the private physician. Their opposition led to a rapid reduction in the scope of the program.

The medical society not only refused to make the application for public health demonstration funds, but so limited the proposals for diagnostic evaluations and referrals that the examining physician would have no responsibility for comprehensiveness of examination, for any advice or information to the patient, or even for referral. At more than a dozen meetings the planner sought to get the original proposal reviewed. He introduced substantial testimony from local, state, and federal public health services in support of its soundness and necessity. But these and other efforts to strengthen the plan were unsuccessful.

The final product, which represented a major emasculation of the original proposal, was submitted to the U.S. Public Health Service for a demonstration grant. The application was rejected. Since the Public Health Service nevertheless indicated that it felt the proposal had a germ of merit, the planner brought medical members of the SPA committee to the government office for a discussion of possible future steps. However, the physician representing the Public Health Service was apparently uninterested in pursuing the matter: he forgot that the meeting had been arranged; came very late; and was totally unfamiliar with the details of the screening proposal.

Another health objective of the San Francisco project was to support adequate rates of welfare reimbursement for chronically ill older persons in order to lay the foundation for an improvement in commercial nursing home services. This objective was seriously threatened when a new director of the state department of finance proposed a reduction in reimbursement rates paid by departments of public welfare to nursing homes. Rates for the San Francisco area would then be substantially below those currently in effect. The project director's knowledge about the inadequacy of existent nursing home care alerted her to the dangerous consequences of this step.

After an informal exploration with the state department of

public welfare, an emergency committee was assembled from various units of the Social Planning Department concerned with health, medical care, and rehabilitation. A representative of the San Francisco Central Labor Union, a hospital administrator, directors of municipal welfare departments, and nursing home operators were subsequently added to the committee or involved in its work. Influential laymen associated with the Social Planning Department, but not directly with the activities of the SPA, were persuaded to make use of their acquaintance with the governor and the director of finance. Meanwhile, the planner accumulated evidence that at the prevailing rate, which exceeded the proposed rate by over 30 percent, more than five hundred older persons qualified for medical assistance were unable to afford the nursing home care which had been recommended for them. This information and the proposed reduction in rates were given wide publicity. Nursing home owners and administrators, and relatives of patients, began calling for further information and protesting the impending reduction. Although they were not prepared to state that they would discharge patients who were currently receiving medical assistance for the aged, various nursing home operators did threaten to reject public assistance patients in the future. Formal communications were forwarded to the governor, to the director of finance, and to legislative representatives. Large numbers of individuals and social agencies were persuaded to make independent protests, and representatives of the SPA's emergency committee testified at a legislative hearing. Ninety days later, *higher* rates of reimbursement were established.

Contra Costa County

At the time the Ford Foundation began its grant program for demonstration projects in planning for the aging, Contra Costa had few social welfare agencies. Most of the voluntary services for the aging were located in the western area. And while most of the older people were concentrated there and in the northern area, there was a noticeable trend toward construction of large "retirement villages" in semirural sectors to the east. The county already boasted 13,000 housing units especially designed for the elderly and was expected to need additional residential facilities for some 25,000 retired persons within the next five years.

The economic and tax base of the county was unevenly distributed. Despite Contra Costa's startling industrial growth in the western and northern areas, agriculture in other sectors of the county remained an important part of its economy. In 1963, 60 percent of the acreage was still used for crop production.

In much of the county, health and welfare services were primarily provided by county government. The county welfare department maintained an extensive social service department; the county hospital had a geriatrics service; the county health department operated five district offices providing health services and nursing care.

Most of the few voluntary social welfare agencies in Contra Costa were less than fourteen years old. But each of the county's three major sections (the heavily industrialized west, the suburban central area, and the rural eastern district) had developed its own social planning organization. The west had a strong and active community planning council with one professional employee and minimal financial support from the United Bay Area Crusade. The central and eastern districts each had weak planning councils which lacked sufficient funds to employ professional staff. Consequently, the planning of programs and services for the elderly was as unbalanced as the county's economic conditions and its population distribution. By 1961 the West Contra Costa Community Welfare Council had already organized a committee on the aging as a standing unit, but the other councils had given no attention to the subject, perhaps because most of the voluntary services for the aging were located in the western area.

The Ford Foundation's solicitation of applications for its program for the aging coincided with an effort to develop a county-wide organization for health and welfare planning. Already in existence were a county development association, a chamber of commerce, a taxpayers' association, a county park and recreational department, and an intermittent county-wide United Fund. The director of the West Contra Costa Council proposed to bring together the one strong and the two weak community welfare councils into one county-wide social planning organization. The West Contra Costa Council applied for a Ford Foundation grant which would permit a doubling of its staff and devotion of time and effort to county-wide consolidation.

During the course of the project the three councils merged into the Contra Costa Council of Community Services, governed by five representatives of each predecessor organization. The differing interests, backgrounds, and conditions of the three sections of the county made it difficult, however, for the new organization to act with consistency. Another problem was the lack of funds. The new council's allocation from the United Bay Area Crusade was 8 cents per capita (a total of $33,000) in 1963 as compared with nearly 30 cents ($215,000) for San Francisco and 18 cents ($170,000) for Alameda County.

The county-wide council's Committee on Aging tried to achieve the following goals in the course of the project:

A. Organization of Planning
  1. Establish the extent to which effective planning can be centralized on a county basis or decentralized to regional or local communities
  2. Develop and test both county-wide and local coordinating

committees, requiring recruitment of leadership from other organizations and the uncovering of latent leadership not yet involved in community activity

3. Merge the one strong council in the west and the relatively weaker councils in the central and eastern parts of the county
4. Engage the major county governmental agencies (health, welfare, housing, and recreation) in the work of the new county council and smooth out relationships with the voluntary agency members
5. Strengthen the decision-making responsibilities of the Community Council's board of directors for county-wide action

B. Private and Public Agency Programs for Older People
1. Increase the volume of public low-cost housing through action of the relevant public housing authorities:
   a) In Richmond
   b) In Martinez
   c) Throughout the county
2. Improve the quality of public housing by persuading public housing authorities to introduce drop-in recreation centers in newly constructed public housing projects
   a) Persuade recreation departments of cities and voluntary agencies to help staff these centers
3. Establish a new county-wide service to provide homemaking and home nursing services to out-of-hospital patients
   a) Secure participation of several agencies (county health department, county hospital, visiting nurses' agencies, heart and cancer associations, and the medical society) to launch such a service
   b) Secure a demonstration grant for initial financing from the U.S. Public Health Service or the state health department
   c) Incorporate a new independent agency to provide this service, with approval from the above agencies and from the board of the County Council of Community Services
4. Consolidate various friendly-visiting programs into one strong county service, to be administered by the local chapter of the American Red Cross
5. Enlarge recreation opportunities for the aged throughout the county

a) Stimulate town recreation departments and voluntary
groups, such as churches and women's clubs, to open
drop-in centers for the elderly

The project director was convinced that success in achieving
goals would require a strong, county-wide social planning
council. She recognized that the strength and leadership of the
newly formed county council which employed her were county-
wide in name only. A fundamental prerequisite for any significant success in the demonstration project, she felt, was the development and strengthening of this group. The uneven distribution of service in the county (rather heavily developed in
the western section, but quite undeveloped in the central and
eastern portions) was reflected in the lay leadership of the
county-wide social planning council. The active leadership
consisted almost exclusively of those who had been prominent
in the West Contra Costa Community Welfare Council prior
to the merger. While they felt a new responsibility for county-
wide social service, the experience and needs of the western
section remained uppermost in their minds. Civic and political
leaders from the other sections of the county were not so involved in this nominally county-wide organization.

In contemplating the need to expand representation in social
planning leadership, the project director conducted a survey of
influential civic figures in order to identify promising recruits
for the project and the council. However, most of these prominent industrialists and social leaders proved to be primarily
concerned with the more immediate needs of their local communities and neighborhoods. Some of those who were interested
in assuming a role of county-wide leadership in social welfare
were particularly reluctant to engage in activities that involved
one general field—the area of the aging. They seemed to feel
that planning for the elderly was the proper domain or function
of old people, and considered themselves "far too young" to
be brought into that role. Consequently, new leadership

proved difficult to recruit. The project director spent many hours calling on various individuals, cajoling, persuading, and encouraging them to take active roles. In each instance she emphasized specific projects for which leadership was needed—the construction of new housing units for the elderly; the establishment of a recreation program; the development of a new home medical care service—rather than basing her appeal on an ephemeral "need for social service leadership." She had some success with this approach, bringing in a retired steel company executive and other businessmen with no previous experience in social welfare activities, a psychiatrist, a rural school superintendent, board members from agencies such as the United Bay Area Crusade and the Junior League, and a few teachers, social workers, and housewives. But even these successes proved to be limited, for in many instances these new "leaders" apparently lost interest and failed to discharge their obligations. Often, for example, committee chairmen failed to attend their own meetings.

Health.—One major objective was to institute homemaker and home nursing services for the elderly. Together with the county health officer the planner determined from *which* social agencies it would be necessary to obtain assent if this undertaking were to be successful. Representatives from each of these organizations—the director of the county welfare department; the director of the geriatric service of the county hospital; executive officers of the voluntary heart and cancer associations; and a social worker from the county medical association—were formed into a special Home Visiting Services Committee.

As the committee began to meet, different views as to the proper approach began to emerge. Some members preferred the creation of a new agency that would bring together nursing and homemaking services; others wanted to expand the separate programs of existing agencies. Some wanted physicians to have a major, direct role in the program; others were skeptical about the extent to which physicians would commit themselves to a new program of home care services. As these differences were being discussed, the project director learned that new federal legislation (the Community Facilities Act) had made funds available through the Public Health Service for out-of-hospital services to the aged. This new federal grant program emphasized the demonstration of unique, experimental techniques for meeting home health needs. With this resource in mind, the project director and the county health officer decided that creation of a single, county-wide agency, combining visiting nurse and homemaker services, would be the most promising choice.

The committee began to draft a grant application, designed to obtain funds for a new agency. The proposal was modified several times to meet persistent objections of the director of the county welfare department, who was eventually satisfied with a version which left him the option of either contracting with the new county-wide agency for services to his clientele or arranging to provide homemakers and visiting nurses through the staff of his own department. When the proposal was approved by the various agency representatives on the Home Visiting Services Committee, it was submitted to the board of the Contra Costa Council of Community Services for endorsement. The proposal met further opposition here, especially from board members from the western area of the county who seemed to prefer an enlargement in the programs of the agencies which already served their region. Nevertheless, the proposal was finally approved following a meeting at which the county health officer and the chairman of the Home Visiting Services Committee arduously defended the plan.

With this endorsement, the application for funds was submitted to the U.S. Public Health Service. While it was pending, the county health officer and the committee chairman took steps to incorporate a new agency for home care, as a *fait accompli*, because they feared that the board of the Contra Costa Council might still withdraw its support at any time. This fear proved to have some basis, for when the initial application was subsequently rejected, the executive director of the Council attempted to disband the Home Visiting Services Committee and to have the entire effort abandoned. Before this could be done, however, the committee was able to complete incorporation of the new agency.

The project director then resumed negotiations with the regional office of the Public Health Service and learned that the federal agency was still interested in the proposal. The major improvement required was a strengthening of provisions for research and evaluation of the demonstration project. A short time later a revised proposal was submitted, and an additional local committee was formed to mobilize further community support for the project. This professional advisory committee, composed of physicians, nurses, and social workers, was chaired by an eminent physician engaged in private practice. While the chairman of this advisory group initially expressed some concern that the proposed home visiting service might be viewed as a form of "creeping socialism," the project director and various committee members were ultimately able to convert his doubts into enthusiastic cooperation and leadership.

Despite these various efforts, the application was turned down once again, apparently because its provisions for research and evaluation of the demonstration project were not considered strong enough. In the meantime, however, the county health officer persuaded the Contra Costa County Board of Supervisors to let him allocate $15,000, from his departmental budget, for the new home visiting service. A full-time director was employed, and a differential fee schedule was established for services to private patients, public welfare recipients, and participants in various health insurance plans.

The home care program began operation, and in the first eight months nearly sixteen hundred persons over sixty-five years of age were served.

Housing.—Another early objective of the Contra Costa project was the construction of low-cost public housing units for the elderly in Richmond and San Pablo, urban communities in the western part of the county. Municipal housing officials claimed that little additional housing for the aged was needed in their cities since less than 6 percent of the population was over sixty-five and the local supply was plentiful. To meet these objections the project director presented recently accumulated evidence concerning inadequacies in the area. Richmond and San Pablo contained two thirds of the population in west Contra Costa; nearly 11 percent of these were over sixty-five years of age (nearly double the average percentage for the county). One in five aged residents was receiving public welfare assistance, a circumstance which in itself suggested that many older persons were unable to afford the rentals charged in commercial housing.

The initial resistance of local housing authorities was slowly overcome as the project director presented these and other facts. Plans for additional public housing were drawn up and readied for approval by city councils and municipal referenda. At this stage the project director brought in members of the Committee on Aging and the board of the Contra Costa Council to testify on behalf of the plans at public hearings. In ensuing referenda campaigns, the public housing was stanchly opposed by local realtors who argued that existing facilities were more than adequate to meet needs. The Contra Costa project conducted a countercampaign, distributing fact sheets to church and civic groups and soliciting votes by telephone and through door-to-door canvasses. New public housing for the elderly was approved in the referendum election in each city.

The project director also sought to promote housing for the

elderly in central and eastern sections of the county by bringing pressure to bear upon the Contra Costa County Housing
Authority. Taking advantage of a scheduled regional conference on housing for the elderly, conducted under the auspices
of the National Council on the Aging, she arranged for many
prominent national figures to attend an additional conference in
Contra Costa the next day. At the same time, she arranged for
the release of results of a recent survey which documented the
need for low-income housing for the elderly. County housing
officials attended both the regional and the local conference—
and apparently felt some pressure, for shortly afterward the
president of the Contra Costa Council telephoned the project
director to ask her to "call off" agitation for public housing.
Nevertheless, agitation continued. After many months the
county housing authority finally authorized a referendum on
housing in the town of Martinez, the county seat. The Committee on Aging mobilized political, business, real estate, health,
and welfare leaders on behalf of their cause, and once again
achieved successful results on election day.

Recreation.—A third general area attacked by the project director was the scarcity of recreational and educational resources
for older persons in Contra Costa. She found, at the beginning
of the Ford project, about a dozen sporadically functioning
senior citizens' groups, sponsored by municipal recreation
departments and by a miscellany of voluntary organizations—a
union, a social agency, and women's clubs. The project director established liaison with these organizations "to get
acquainted with personnel, facilities, and resources, to stimulate and inform individuals and groups, and to begin to establish good working relationships with as many persons as possible." She found them relatively satisfied with their limited program of occasional card-playing and partying. She also found
them to be suspicious of her intentions because she was associated with "welfare" and was not a local resident. She tried to

counter these reactions by a conscious effort to identify with their day-to-day interests. She also provided written materials and other information about adult education, library resources, and various experimental programs. She invited these local groups to attend Bay area meetings and arranged for a Ford Foundation consultant and members of the State Advisory Committee on Aging to speak at local meetings. When the state legislature initiated a program of matching funds for local services to the elderly, the news was immediately relayed to these groups.

These general educational efforts produced no tangible results, so the project director concentrated on the recreation department in the city of Richmond. Here a local committee on the aging had long been trying to promote a senior citizen center in the downtown area where a large number of older persons resided. Recreation department staff responded positively to the project director's ideas about leisure-time programs. Moreover, the Richmond housing authority was willing to provide space in one of its new projects for a recreation center for the elderly. The major remaining task was to find funds for matching a state grant so that a program could be financed. This modest sum was rather easily obtained from the Richmond city council and several local civic service organizations.

The final steps were to develop a program proposal in order to secure the demonstration grant from the state and then to assume administrative responsibility for the program if it should come into being. A special committee was formed for this purpose, including local manufacturers and merchants and representatives of service clubs and senior citizens' organizations. The technical services for drafting the proposal were provided by the project director, who engaged in numerous contacts with officials in the state department of welfare. A grant of $11,000 was secured—sufficient to provide space for the program, pay a part-time recreation director, and train a corps of volunteers. Within a year of its opening more than twelve hundred persons were participating each month in the programs at the Richmond recreation center.

The success of the Richmond center stimulated interest in other parts of the county. Other municipal recreation departments and several women's clubs soon applied for state matching grants to finance local recreation programs. This momentum was further reinforced by the project director's organization of the Bay Area Workshop for recreational personnel in which staff from nine communities in Contra Costa County participated.

Denver

Colorado has pioneered in the development of state-wide pensions and health care for the elderly, encouraged in part by the effectiveness of the National Annuity League in influencing state legislation in the field of the aging. The state's old age assistance program is more like a pension than a public assistance program, and was one of the first to provide extensive funds for medical care to nearly the entire aged population of a state.

Denver, the state capital, and regional center for the entire Rocky Mountain area, has a typical metropolitan complex of public and voluntary service agencies, located primarily in the central city. At the time of the Ford grant, the Metropolitan Council for Community Service (MCCS) was the recognized social welfare planning agency, although the independent Senior Citizens' Council (SCC), the Mayor's Commission on Aging, a state commission, and the National Annuity League were also involved to some extent in planning.

The concern of the MCCS (formerly the Denver Area Welfare Council) for the needs of the elderly dated back to at least

1949 when it sponsored a meeting of clergymen to discuss problems of the aging. In 1950 the MCCS completed a study on this subject for the Denver area, and subsequently organized a one-day conference for representatives of business and labor on employment problems of the elderly. A continuing Committee on Aging was established in 1952 to address itself to health, recreation, and housing needs. In 1953 this committee urged the governor to appoint a state commission on aging, and in the same year it became incorporated as the SCC.

The SCC was provided with staff by the Welfare Council until 1959 when the two agencies severed relationships. While the SCC was established to organize and coordinate the service needs of senior citizen clubs, the MCCS also suggested that it could "make its contribution to the community and play its part in the over-all objectives of community planning and service." As a result, the SCC had begun to function in a dual capacity: coordinating the efforts of various organizations of the elderly; and, by 1960, often providing interpretations of "the needs of the elderly" that contradicted the interpretations of the MCCS.

Denver, therefore, had several organizations involved to some extent in planning for the elderly. The Ford Foundation project was seen by the sponsors as an opportunity to develop planning for the aged in the area. The MCCS proposed to join with the SCC as an equal partner in a demonstration which was soon called the Metropolitan Planning Project for Older People (MPPOP). As the project unfolded, the project director's offices were located in the quarters of the MCCS, and the bulk of his associations were with the professional staff and lay members of this organization. However, it was necessary for him to handle the tension between the MCCS's belief in balanced development on all fronts in health and welfare and the SCC's paramount interest in the needs of the elderly.

At one time or another the Denver project tried to achieve the following goals:

A. Arrangements for Central Planning for the Aged in Denver
   1. Improve the relationship between the MCCS and the SCC
      a) Appoint the president of the SCC as vice chairman of the MPPOP
      b) Coordinate the activities of the SCC and the MPPOP
      c) Merge the SCC and the MPPOP
      d) Secure the appointment of the president of the SCC as the next chairman of the merged planning unit
      e) Secure an MCCS commitment to provide full-time staff service for the aging after the termination of the demonstration
   2. Improve relationships between the United Fund and the MCCS
B. Relationships among Direct-Service Agencies
   1. Organize a conference of nonprofit homes for the elderly
   2. Organize a conference group of agencies servicing the chronically ill aged
   3. Establish a friendly working relationship between the Denver housing authority and the MCCS
   4. Encourage closer cooperation among Jewish-sponsored social agencies
C. Quality of Existing Programs for the Elderly
   1. Enrich the programs of nonprofit housing corporations serving the aged
      a) Secure participation of housing managers in training institutes, stressing the social needs of residents
      b) Provide various technical aides to enhance occupancy of such homes by needy aged persons
   2. Persuade the Denver housing authority to build more units of low-cost public housing and to introduce social services in their management
   3. Induce selected agencies to initiate an organized home medical care program
   4. Induce certain health agencies to initiate a program of preventive services

5. Persuade similar agencies to introduce comprehensive rehabilitation programs into commercial nursing homes
6. Expand preretirement educational programs through selected
   industries and the Adult Education Association
7. Persuade the family service agencies to increase their allocation of caseworkers for counseling the aged
8. Persuade the Denver recreation department to service a
   federation of senior citizen clubs
9. Persuade the Allied Jewish Council to support family counseling for older clients

The broad goal of "strengthening central planning for the
aged" was the focus of much of the Denver project director's
efforts. In pursuance of his charge he established a special
committee to evaluate the functions and relationships among
the Mayor's Commission on Aging, the Governor's Commission
on Aging, and particularly the two organizations which were
jointly sponsoring the Ford project—the MCCS and the SCC.
At the outset he posed a series of questions, designed to clarify
the relationship of these separate planning and coordinating
agencies to each other and to various direct-service social
agencies in the Denver metropolitan area. Why had the SCC
been organized? What had the MCCS envisioned as the SCC's
role when it had encouraged its formation? What had been the
SCC's impact upon services to the aging? What attention had
the MCCS given to the needs of the aging since the creation of
the SCC? What were sources of dissatisfaction in relations between the MCCS and the SCC? And so on.

Although the study of arrangements for central planning had
been a major reason for the existence of the demonstration
project, the planner soon found that the various parties were
not particularly eager to pursue these questions. Neither the
SCC nor the MCCS would firmly acknowledge that any problems or conflicting aims or responsibilities existed. Yet, at the
same time, there were those within each organization who believed that *it* should have primary responsibility and that the

other should play a secondary role. The chairman of the SCC, a retired educator, held very strong convictions about the neglect of the aging in the Denver area, and felt that their needs could only receive appropriate attention if the independent position of the SCC could be protected; he feared (with good reason) that explorations of a "central planning responsibility" in Denver would pose a threat to the current status of his organization—might result in subordination of it to the MCCS planning council.

On the other hand, the MCCS expected to have the leading role in central planning. The situation was further complicated by relations between the executive director of the Mile High (United) Fund and the director of the MCCS. The Fund, continually needing to better the results of its annual drives, was eager to hold the line against expanding its area of responsibility —giving most of its attention to the central city. The MCCS, on the other hand, favored a metropolitan planning function. While the MCCS wished to expand, the Fund was reluctant to underwrite this. At the same time, the MCCS regretted the fact that, in this context of limited finances for planning, the Fund was giving the SCC money which the latter was using to pay planning staff. The MCCS, then, hardly wished to see the SCC play a dominant role—if roles were to be reevaluated and coordinated.

Despite this background of conflicts and strains, the project director was committed to the premise that a single, central planning organization for the aging was the only practical outcome of efforts to reconcile planning roles in Denver. He persisted in putting forward his views as to the need for central coordination, pressing his questions, and drawing upon external data to support his position—monographs by experts in community planning, reports from the White House Conference on Aging, and other sources in health and welfare planning. These appeals had little effect. He then brought to bear the influence of a number of lay members of the MCCS in an attempt to convince the chairman of the SCC that a single, consolidated arrangement would have advantages for the SCC. Over a period of six months a number of persons met with the SCC chairman, persuaded and argued with him, in an attempt to make him see (as the project director expressed it) "the validity of one planning unit, regardless of where it might be located." Apparently, these efforts had sufficient impact upon the chairman to produce a frame of mind in which he would sit down and discuss the "possibility of deactivating SCC and what this might mean to sharpened planning for the aging." He met with the executive director of the MCCS and the chairman of the Council's committee on aging. The MCCS director proposed that the SCC merge with his own organization and suggested that its chairman could assume the chairmanship of the combined operation, thus putting him "in a position to influence the stronger resources of the MCCS for the objectives in which he believed . . . . to support the interests of people like himself, committed to the aging."

In ensuing months, the project director and the SCC chairman had a number of contacts, some in a social context, in which the latter became increasingly reassured that the MCCS would genuinely support planning efforts to cope with the needs of the elderly. Ultimately, the chairman himself presented to his organization a proposal for an SCC-MCCS merger, and played a strong role in overcoming remaining opposition. Consolidation was approved, although the SCC retained its charter of incorporation to guard against the possibility that the merger might not be lasting. At the end of the Ford demonstration project, the SCC returned to the MCCS. The Mile High Fund terminated its independent allocation to the SCC, and provided funds for MCCS staff services for planning for the elderly, on an indefinite basis.

Health.—One of the goals of the Denver project was to improve services to the chronically ill elderly, particularly through better coordination of existing services and through development of a program of home care services. At that time there was no organization or mechanism for bringing together the many public and private agencies and interests involved in programs and services having to do with this problem. The project director invited representatives from forty-five separate health and social welfare agencies to a general meeting for discussion of chronic illness and the possibilities of coordination and development of services. Interest was sufficiently strong at this meeting to produce agreement to establish a Conference Group on Chronic Disease and Rehabilitation. A temporary steering committee, consisting of four physicians (three in public health and one in private practice), a public health nurse, a social worker, a nursing home operator, and a state public welfare official, was formed to explore possibilities of "coordination in chronic illness."

Although the Conference Group met many times, little was accomplished. The project director, with the aid of a health consultant, developed a proposal for four programs which the Conference might undertake: a comprehensive home care service; the introduction of rehabilitation services in commercial nursing homes; a community-wide program of preventive health services; and a central office to provide service information to physicians who encountered patients with particularly complex, chronic conditions. But most of the forty-five (later sixty) separate agencies involved in the Conference Group raised practical reservations concerning each of these proposals, and the project director, not a specialist in health planning, was unable to offer solutions to these problems. Extensive discussions were held at several meetings, but the only result was the appointment of an eminent private physician as chairman of the Conference.

The project director persisted in his efforts by bringing in a nationally known specialist in the field of chronic-illness planning to address the group. He provided practical suggestions and examples of feasible approaches for developing programs and interagency coordination. Apparently this meeting had some impact upon several state health officials who were in attendance, for the following day the Colorado health department offered the Conference Group some demonstration funds for a pilot information-referral service for the chronically ill in Denver. The offer was accepted, and the service was established for a four-month demonstration period with state health department funds (secured by an application from the MCCS), supplemented by contributions of administrative expenses from the Colorado Tuberculosis Association, the county medical society, and the Western Geriatric Society (a statewide association of nursing homes).

In general, the Conference Group became rather aimless. The special interests of various steering committee members began to emerge, and diversity rather than unity and coherence became a dominant characteristic of the Conference Group. The project director had emphasized a "problem-centered focus" at the outset, in order to overcome diversity; but he was unable to maintain common interest with specific enough proposals to sustain a program, or even a feeling of common purpose. He finally recognized that he was not "equipped to provide the clarity of professional direction that might have helped unite the committee. For the most part, there was a groping rather than a sharpness of direction in the staff contribution." Moreover, the urgency of many other planning efforts made it difficult for him to develop sufficient technical expertise. As time went on, the rivalries and conflicting interests of the committee members and dissatisfaction with the project director undermined any attempt at cohesive action. Plans for a proposal to the U.S. Public Health Service, to obtain funds for a long-term information-referral service, were abandoned. As the Ford demonstration came to an end, it was concluded that "there is little agreement within the committee regarding a program of action to be recommended."

Housing.—The planner's attention was directed to improving managerial techniques and services in various housing projects in which older persons resided. He brought together, as the Conference of Nonprofit Housing for the Aging, representatives of a dozen apartment house projects for the elderly recently constructed in Denver. They held a series of meetings to exchange their practical experiences in managing special facilities for the aged. In the course of these conferences, and as he further familiarized himself with housing facilities for the aging throughout the city, he became aware of a number of recurring problems. Managerial problems included: inability to recruit occupants and maintain a high percentage of residency; difficulties in handling health and personal problems of older persons; uncertainties about taxation and other legal matters associated with the operation of a nonprofit corporation. A number of tenant problems were also apparent. Residents who became infirm or disabled were unable to get appropriate medical attention at home and were not being transported elsewhere. Older persons felt cut off from familiar and conventional forms of recreation that were not available in the special projects. Underlying the problems encountered by tenants was the issue of the extent of a project manager's responsibility. Should he limit himself to a conventional management-tenant relationship, or look upon the elderly residents as persons for whom he was responsible in all or most facets of their day-to-day living situations?

The project director proceeded to inform himself about these various issues and provided useful information to the housing group. He arranged for: a study of the characteristics of residents in local projects, conducted by the University of Denver, to provide a foundation for effective planning to meet their requirements; the publication of a professionally designed brochure to attract new tenants; collection and interpretation of tax regulations for nonprofit corporations, and a special meeting between the nonprofit housing group and the state tax exemption commission; the maintenance of central files on housing legislation; and provision of information about health and welfare community agencies which housing managers could call upon to aid their tenants. To provide technical knowledge, to open channels of communication to national resources, and to enhance the prestige of the group, the project director also arranged for the National Council on the Aging to hold a regional conference on nonprofit housing for the elderly, in Denver.

Recreation.—Prior to its merger with the MCCS, the SCC had provided federated membership for some forty senior citizens' clubs. Most of these clubs were quite content to function with very limited programs. Nevertheless, they seemed to miss the additional social activity which had resulted from the SCC affiliation. The Ford project director attempted to develop a recreational program for these clubs, on a federated basis, and eventually tried to get the Denver department of parks and recreation to sponsor it. A general proposal for staffing was presented to the department, but was quickly rejected.

A year later the Ford project created a task force on leisure-time services. During three months of study a carefully detailed recreation program for senior citizens' clubs was outlined, specifying objectives and detailing the staff time and costs which the city would be expected to assume. This new, quite specific proposal was presented to the department of parks by an influential layman and social service agency representatives. The project director provided the department with technical information as to the means for organizing a program, and the MCCS explicitly indicated that it would endorse the department's total program if this program for the elderly were incorporated. The municipal agency responded favorably to these overtures, with the result that more than thirty clubs had refederated by the spring of 1964 and were participating in a varied program staffed by the department of parks and recreation.

Worcester

Public concern for the health and welfare of the elderly in Worcester dates at least from 1948. In that year the Worcester State Hospital reported that persons over sixty-five years of age represented 30 percent of all admissions, a fact which, in the view of the hospital officials, reflected "a failure of the community to supply services in the city which would render such hospitalization unnecessary for many." The YWCA lobby was being used as a resting place and social center for innumerable older women who were obviously socially deprived. In 1949, several organizations opened a social center for older people, which functioned as a recreational center two afternoons a week. In time, the department of public welfare, the United Fund, and the YWCA also became interested in the problems of the elderly. The Community Chest and Council (later the Community Services of Greater Worcester) appointed a Committee on Aging to broaden the base of interest and support for programs to the aging. In the years between 1952 and 1960 this committee organized six senior citizens' hobby shows and four conferences on aging; contributed testimony to state and federal legislative hearings; and participated in an intercity study of the needs of retired workers. Most visibly and permanently, the committee brought into being the demonstration Information Service for the Aging, which, while lacking funds, was staffed by volunteer personnel from eighteen health and welfare agencies and by volunteer receptionists furnished by about twenty church and civic groups. The board of public welfare was seeking to develop a program of boarding care for the elderly, the Jewish Family Service was pioneering by offering the services of case aides to the elderly, and the Salvation Army had already set up a drop-in lounge for the elderly which functioned throughout the week. Against this background of progress in planning for the elderly, in a community where little money could be found for developing programs and services, the Ford Foundation made a demonstration grant to the Committee on Aging of the Planning Council within Community Services of Greater Worcester.

The major purpose of the Worcester project was simply to expand services for the aged by working through already established agencies. This led to attempts to achieve a variety of objectives at different times:

A. Organization of a Multiservice Center for the Elderly
  1. Persuade the Golden Rule (United) Fund and the Community Services of Greater Worcester to support and sponsor such a center—later converted into an effort to establish an independent corporation, without ties to the Fund
  2. Persuade any of several agencies (YWCA, housing authority, department of parks) to provide space for the center
  3. Secure initial financing from any of the following: United Fund; department of public health; private donors; or, in the last resort, as the contribution of volunteer staff time
B. Medical Care
  1. Introduce recreational therapy, as a first step in rehabilitation, into several proprietary nursing homes
  2. Secure a sponsoring agency to administer recreational therapy —either the Community Services of Greater Worcester, the YMCA, or the Bay State Rehabilitation Society
  3. Secure the cooperation of five nursing home owners
  4. Secure initial financing from the public health service or from the nursing home operators themselves
  5. Increase the state welfare department's reimbursements to nursing homes for patients on public welfare
C. Casework and Personal Counseling
  1. Persuade the Family Service Association to assign casework

staff to work with older clients and train the rest of the staff
to recognize the needs of such clients
2. Continue the volunteer work of the Information Service for
the Aging by securing new volunteers
3. Incorporate the information service in the proposed multi-
purpose center
4. Train volunteers for a friendly visiting service
D. Housing
1. Persuade the housing authority to construct low-cost housing
in a downtown location suitable for the most needy aged
persons
2. Induce the housing authority to include a center for recreation for the aged in a new, low-rent apartment house project

The project in Worcester was funded explicitly for the purpose of demonstrating what a full-time planner could accomplish in getting social agencies to expand and improve their
services to the elderly. In the course of the project, however,
the creation of an independent multiservice center for the
aging came to be a central goal of planning efforts. Much of the
explanation for this fundamental change in emphasis lies in the
general nature of welfare planning in Worcester and the particular circumstances surrounding the sponsorship of the project.

The Worcester Committee on Aging (WCA), to which the
project director was assigned, and its parent organization,
Community Services, were in conflict throughout the project.
The committee, chaired by a prominent physician, had long
been an active and dedicated force promoting the cause of the
aging in Worcester, but it did not have strong support from
Worcester's Community Services. While some members of the
WCA were socially and economically prominent in the community, they were not members of the smaller coterie which
dominated the policy of the Golden Rule (United) Fund and
the Planning Council. In the almost ten years it had existed,

the WCA had repeatedly found the Fund and the Council unwilling to endorse a significant investment of funds in either new or expanded services for the aging. By the time the Ford project began, the WCA, and its chairman especially, was thoroughly convinced that only limited progress in the field of aging could be made in Worcester unless a new base, essentially independent of the Fund and the Council, could be established. The creation of a multiservice center was seen as a means to this end—the establishment of a new organization which could develop services as they were needed, and ultimately secure financial support in the community by dramatically demonstrating effectiveness. But the Ford project director, while serving as staff to the committee, was actually an employee of Community Services. Moreover, he adhered to the conventional view that the function of a planning committee is not directly to develop and sponsor programs and services, but to stimulate other organizations to do so. Nevertheless, the project director's views did not prevail, and much of the Worcester project's efforts were invested in the establishment of a multiservice center.

An early aspect of efforts to establish the new center was determination of a suitable and available site to house the program. Several board members of the YWCA who were active on the WCA suggested that space might be available in a new "Y" building, already being constructed in a desirable downtown location. The project director and the committee chairman responded favorably to this proposal but soon found that several board members of the "Y" were opposed to the idea. It was apparent that the issue would not be quickly resolved.

Several other possible sites for the center came to the attention of the project director in the following weeks. The Salvation Army, which was already operating a rather limited drop-in program for the elderly, proffered space, but its offers of cooperation and facilities were continually rebuffed. On one occasion, the chairman of the WCA took every opportunity to dissuade project committee members from including the Salvation Army in a planning group for the multiservice center. As a guest speaker at an annual meeting of the Army, he gave a forceful talk on the need of a center for the elderly in Worcester, without acknowledging the fact that the Salvation Army was already operating one. So far as it is possible to tell, the WCA's constant rejection of cooperation from the Salvation Army stemmed from a fear that the latter's poor standing in social welfare circles in Worcester would be a serious liability in the attempt to develop a successful new program.

Another possibility explored by the WCA was the chance that the Worcester housing authority might make space available in one of its public housing projects. The project director and committee members examined several possible sites, but regarded them as unsatisfactory because they were not easily accessible to a great many of the older persons who were expected to use the planned services. Several park department sites were visited too, but were rejected because they were located in "undesirable" neighborhoods. Subsequently, members of the WCA went to see the executive director of the housing authority to find out if current plans for new projects included a more favorably located project near downtown, and if the multiservice program might obtain space in it. They found that while the authority was contemplating additional construction of units for the elderly, these were planned as "garden" apartments in outlying sections of the city. Moreover, it was opposed to using public housing facilities for a social service center. The authority's director was unresponsive to WCA attempts to persuade him. He not only refused to consider the possibility of providing a site for the center program, but was firmly opposed to the construction of downtown housing for the elderly, on the grounds that older persons prefer to live in other parts of the city.

Over the course of several years, the WCA was finally able to obtain space in the new "Y" building. When other possibilities failed to materialize, the project director put aside his earlier hesitance to combat the opposing elements on the "Y" board. He engaged in a series of cooperative meetings with the executive director of the "Y" and spent many hours in conferring with members of the WCA, particularly those who were also on the board of the "Y." When the issue was put to the test, near the end of the Ford project, elements of resistance proved to be rather easily overcome.

A major requisite for establishing the new center, of course, was funds for staff, rent, and other expenses. With this need in view, the WCA arranged for the incorporation of the Age Center of Worcester Area as the legal vehicle for the multiservice program. A proposal for an allocation from the United Fund was submitted to the Planning Council of Worcester's Community Services. Prospects for a favorable response were not promising since the Council consistently gave low ratings to programs and services to meet the needs of the elderly. The multiservice center proposal was briefly reviewed and tabled for a period of several months. When the project director persistently inquired about prospects for the center, he was told that "the matter has been submitted to further study." When the Planning Council finally submitted an evaluation of the multiservice program to the Fund for review in its allocation decisions, the priority rating given to the center proposal was too far down the list of "worthy causes" to come even close to being given serious consideration for financing from the limited budget of the Golden Rule Fund.

In addition to the financial problems posed by this rejection from the Fund, other consequences soon became evident. The knowledge of this failure to support the center deterred the "Y" from offering space in its new building as a location for program operations. The Junior League of Worcester had shown

interest in providing volunteer manpower for some of the services in the projected program, but did not follow through when
the Fund's opposition became known.

Eventually, however, the Golden Rule Fund sanctioned
efforts by the Age Center to seek support from other sources in
the community. The Center corporation established a special
fund-raising committee, chaired by the president of a local
bank who also served as a director of the United Fund. Negotiations were undertaken with a firm of fund-raising specialists,
and plans were made for a local drive. But the fund-raising
firm was "scared off" from this assignment. When one of its
representatives came to Worcester to consider seriously a final
contract, the chairman of the center's fund-raising committee
presented a discouraging picture in the course of a brief interview in which he indicated that his bank was not going to be
able to contribute to the project "for several years." Ultimately,
however, with the help of a former mayor of Worcester and an
old-line Yankee family involved throughout in WCA and Age
Center activities, a successful drive was launched. The support
of these and other individuals helped to counter discourage-
ments by members of the United Fund, and several thousand
dollars were acquired.

The key factor in the Age Center's efforts to secure funds
was a successful application for a demonstration grant from the
U.S. Public Health Service. With a special "project writing"
grant from the Massachusetts department of health, the center
was able to hire a prominent medical consultant to frame a
project proposal which effectively blended the many elements
and interests in aging in Worcester—the existent information
service; a small grant from the state health department; a training program for friendly visitors; the support of the Worcester
Council of Churches, the city manager, the local press, the
state nursing home association, the YWCA, and other activities
and organizations—into a relatively impressive record of local

preparedness to support a multiservice center for the aging. When the Public Health Service expressed interest in the project proposal, Worcester's Community Services also expressed some indications of support and endorsement.

Shortly after the termination of the Ford project, the Age Center received a demonstration-research grant from the Public Health Service which enabled it to begin operation in the new YWCA building. The character of the program was somewhat altered from original plans because of the need to emphasize service for chronically ill older persons in order to meet qualifications for a health demonstration grant. The center was staffed by a medical social worker, a public health nurse, a physiatrist, a nutritionist, and a recreational therapist, as well as a full-time executive director and a number of volunteers. Several months after the program began, the Age Center was not only serving as a center for health and social services, but was also undertaking a special experimental demonstration in providing consultation to local nursing homes in an effort to help them enrich their programs in care and rehabilitation.

INTERMEDIATE GOALS IN
SOCIAL PLANNING

As the lists of objectives in the various Ford projects indicate, most of the goals developed in the course of the planning projects embodied proposals for changes in the policies of organizations rather than for alterations in fundamental societal systems or in human attitudes or behavior patterns. These were goals of the type referred to in the preceding chapter as "preference" goals. For the most part, they emerged from attempts to find relatively concrete approaches for attaining broad objectives, such as "improving housing for the elderly." In turn, they often led to the posing of many extremely specific goals, such as "obtaining an appointment with the director of the housing authority."

The very broadest and the most specific measures were frequently considered quite extensively and established explicitly before investments of planning resources were made in attempts to achieve them. More often than not their feasibility and usefulness were weighed, and alternatives were examined and rejected.

The intermediate goals, calling for changes in organizational policies, were usually implicit preferences. Attempts to achieve these intermediate or preference goals occupied most of the time and energy of the project directors. Even so, these objectives were often developed in the course of planning activity, without explicit consideration and identification. In some instances it only became apparent that they were goals, in fact, because so much was being done to achieve them. And yet, it is the explicit consideration and expression of these goals that is essential to effective planning—that distinguishes *planning* from less systematic and less successful types of efforts to improve social conditions and that makes it feasible. Explicit consideration of intermediate aims ensures that specific measures are pertinent to achieving the very general, desired objectives.

The absence of explicit, carefully analyzed and developed intermediate goals is characteristic not only of social planning efforts, but of most goal-oriented activity. "Goals or final objectives of governmental organizations and activity are usually formulated in very general and ambiguous terms—'justice,' 'the general welfare,' or 'liberty.' " [7] As Banfield has suggested:

Organizations . . . . do not generally have ends which are concrete enough in content to provide an unambiguous criterion by which to choose among the competing advantages associated with

[7] Simon, *Administrative Behavior: a Study of Decision-making Processes in Administrative Organizations*, p. 5.

the various diagnostic criteria. . . . Often, organizational objectives exist only as vague generalities.[8]

This ambiguity in goals is not without its constructive and functional aspects. Fitch offers some insight in observing that "in the mixed societies, with both public and private sectors, and numerous power groups with differing objectives, the political problem is one of achieving a resolution of conflicting claims which will be generally acceptable." [9] Ambiguous goals not only permit the avoidance of conflict among interest groups and organizations but are also useful in permitting planners to avoid a preference ranking among conflicting values, to seek, "with equal force, goods which in nature or human nature are negatively correlated; glory without hazard, security without constraint, stable markets without government interference—and so on." [10] There is one other, very practical function of this ambiguity. Planners are often expected to act with more certainty in the recommendations they put forth than is wholly warranted by present knowledge. This has led Gouldner to observe that one of the most guarded organizational secrets of professionals is the lack of sufficient technical knowledge:

When we begin to raise questions about evidence, about proof firm and hard, proof clear and consistent, proof public and examinable, concerning the decisions of welfare agencies we begin to enter into . . . the area of the dark secret . . .

The general question is: Where is the evidence in this and in a thousand other cases that would justify, in some rational way, the preference for a particular procedure, policy, or program? [11]

[8] Banfield, "The Decision-making Schema," *Public Administration Review,* XVII (1957), 279.

[9] Fitch, "Organization for Planning and Development of Metropolitan Areas," in *Social Problems of Development and Urbanization,* Vol. VII, Science and Technology for Development, United States Papers prepared for the United Nations Conference on the application of science and technology for the benefit of the less developed areas, p. 55.

[10] Seeley, "Central Planning: Prologue to a Critique," in Morris, ed., *Centrally Planned Change,* p. 46.

[11] Gouldner, "The Secrets of Organizations," in *The Social Welfare Forum, 1963,* p. 167.

The tendency for goals to remain vague and ambiguous has costly consequences for planning efforts. The lack of more concrete goals leaves the planner without a guide which can provide coherence and cohesion to his day-to-day actions. He lacks clarity about the ways in which single acts lead perceptibly to resolution or reduction of social problems and to the realization of preamble goals. He lacks a sense of direction about the progression from a small-scale demonstration to massive programs. He has little indication of personnel and funds required and the social institutions which are involved at successive stages. In the absence of explicit intermediate goals, planners often tend to view specific acts as guides to their overall efforts. Sometimes actions taken primarily because of a faith that they are somehow appropriate become the major focus of the planner's attention regardless of their utility and relevance.

Intermediate goals are relatively concrete, yet they are sufficiently general to provide a foundation for decision. If they are explicitly identified and analyzed, they can serve as frameworks for ascertaining whether specific actions are useful or relevant. They can be maps to which planners can refer to see if they are on the road to their ultimate destinations. This is because they reflect the relative feasibility of a planning effort.

IV · THE DYNAMICS OF
GOAL DEVELOPMENT

In addition to being possible solutions to social problems, goals are also composite products of personal, professional, and institutional values; identified dissatisfactions; motives for seeking changes; diagnoses of social problems; and information of varying qualities and quantities. They are guides used by planners for decisions and actions, as well as for desired objectives.

In the type of planning with which we are concerned, involving attempts to change the policies of organizations, the intermediate or preference goals determine ensuing events and actions. They are the starting point for any attempt to understand the efforts of a planner as he tries to overcome organizational resistance. However, the dynamic importance of a goal cannot be clear without some consideration of those aspects of planning that precede its development. Identification and analysis of the significance of all such factors defy human comprehension, although some of the more important developmental components of a preference goal can be briefly considered.

WHEN DOES PLANNING BEGIN?

If we were truly to consider all the factors that are an integral part of the development of a preference goal, the range of phenomena we would be required to include would be prohibitively infinite. Indeed, in the strictest sense we would at least need to lay before us the entire history of mankind, examine the workings of the individual mind, and, perhaps, contemplate the origin and nature of the universe. Even if we were to limit our attention to the major ingredients of the kinds of planning with which we are concerned—social welfare planners, the needs they desire to meet, and the organizations whose policies they try to change—we would find ourselves in a position where we would have to undertake such tasks as the psychoanalysis of each and every planner. We would be interested in finding out as much as we could about the planner's social and psychological background, the character and extent of his training, his social and political views and perceptions, his emotional responses to a variety of situations, the extent of his knowledge, and the circumstances confronting him prior to and during goal development.

A more useful approach is to limit our observations to the sequence of events beginning with that point in time, space, or course of events when a planning effort is initiated. This would not be the point at which a project is officially undertaken, a goal is proclaimed, or an intent is announced. Rather, it would be the point which distinguishes planning from nonplanning efforts and events.

Since planning is an attempt to solve problems, a major ingredient in the development of a planning effort is dissatisfaction. To be sure, every planner is not necessarily dissatisfied with current or anticipated conditions. As an employee, a planner may work to change something which he likes as it is. But even so, he is serving as an agent of a dissatisfied party.

While this dissatisfaction may have several roots, in social welfare it is customary to think in unselfish terms. An early project report from Worcester relates:

During 1948 it became apparent to several unassociated individuals in wholly different milieus in Worcester that the astonishing growth of population in the upper age levels must be accompanied by expanded community services. . . . The very earliest recognition came from the Worcester State Hospital. Its stepped up admissions of the over-60 age group (30 percent) were attributed to the failure of the community to supply services which would render hospitalization unnecessary for many.

But dissatisfaction of a different order also exists. In Denver, it was generated by the competition of two city-wide organizations for resources with which to plan.

Both councils served metropolitan Denver and employed full-time staff with funds supplied by the Mile High Fund. The overlapping of planning functions for the aging was a core problem to be dealt with. . . . In many people's minds, and at times in the minds of some on the Senior Citizens' Council board, the demonstration was a Metropolitan Council instrument to take over the Senior Citizens' Council.

In Contra Costa a mixture of dissatisfactions led to the planning project. The population of aged had increased four-fold in twenty years, and was expected to double again in the next seven years; already a sixth of the elderly were receiving Old Age Assistance and were in hospitals or nursing homes. At the same time, the county's three planning councils lacked a firm foundation of leadership.

Even though dissatisfaction is an ingredient common to all planning, that alone is not sufficient to mark the starting point of a planning sequence. Dissatisfaction does not, in itself, differentiate planners from nonplanners. Dreamers, malcontents, and social critics, as well as planners, are dissatisfied with a state of affairs, but the planner is actually committed to working for change, regardless of the character and extent of his commitment. Another distinctive characteristic is his use of the best available knowledge and insight as to cause and effect, means and end, action and reaction, as guides for his decisions and actions.

THE DECISION TO INTERVENE

A commitment to change is the genesis of a planning endeavor. Unless someone has a hand in altering events in accordance with his commitment, social change can only be said to be a configuration of events, occurrences, and developments. The configuration may be attributable to, or associated with, some great force underlying the nature and functioning of the universe, some natural law of economic, social, political, and physical development, or merely random events. Without the presence of some human commitment to social change it is not possible to say that planning has taken place. No actor can be said to be solving problems, changing, or intervening—whether rationally or otherwise—unless he can be said to be more than caught up in events. In Denver, for example, some dissatisfaction was expressed by the Metropolitan Council for Community Service as early as 1949, but no planning emerged until 1959 when the Council committed itself to improving services to the aged in order to secure a Ford Foundation grant.

Commitment begins when concern with conditions of social welfare is expressed positively rather than negatively. The San Francisco project was dissatisfied, for example, with existing arrangements for the medical care of elderly persons. The project determined to work for "the enhancement of the health, medical care, and rehabilitation of elderly persons of San Francisco." This kind of statement begins the identification of targets for change, matters to be "improved." In Contra Costa there was concern about the 20 percent of the aged whose incomes were inadequate for the purchase of decent housing. This became converted into the goal of building low-cost public housing. In Denver dissatisfaction with the competition between two planning agencies was replaced with a determination to coordinate or merge the two.

If intentions to intervene reflect some commitment, little can be assumed about its nature and extent, dimensions which in the last analysis are the only relevant and reliable indices of what the commitment will mean in later stages of planning. The decision to intervene must be considered in conjunction with the motives that lead to it. This is not to suggest that such motives are easy to detect, but it is possible to isolate a number of kinds of motives to which the analyst can be sensitive. At least four different kinds of motives, singly or in combinations, can lead to a decision to intervene to improve conditions of social welfare.

First, a planner (or his employer) may undertake to bring about social change out of a concern for the needs of human beings. This motive may be embodied in a commitment to a quite specific change which the planner is confident would result in improvement of the welfare of specified individuals or of a particular segment of society. Or, it may be reflected in a vague desire to disrupt the *status quo*, based upon the conviction that any change is "a change for the better"—that a disturbance of the present equilibrium is more likely to lead toward, or result in, an eventual improvement than not.

A second type of motive which may lead a planner to commit himself to bringing about social change is a desire to learn from experience and experimentation. A demonstration or pilot venture may be undertaken primarily for the intrinsic knowledge to be gleaned as to the nature of social change endeavors and the factors and circumstances involved. Or, it may be undertaken to lay the groundwork for future, perhaps larger-scale, versions of the same approach. For a planner who acts on this type of motive, the experimental nature of the effort is primary; the extent to which the change is realized is incidental or secondary. The planner's major interest is to do things in a way that will facilitate learning. It is not often, however, that this motive is truly dominant. Much of the time a demonstration is organized to prove a point about which planners are convinced from their own experience or that of others. Moreover, a social planner's devotion to alleviating human distress often leads him to deviate from the experimental model.

Third, a planner may decide to intervene in response to varying kinds and degrees of constraints upon him to do so. Left alone, his response to a proposed change may range from indifference to vigorous opposition. But various forms of influence—legal authority, persuasion, cajolery, inducements—may lead him to alter his natural inclination, to transcend his indifference, or subordinate his opposition. Since the purported reason for his employment is to improve conditions of social welfare, he is especially sensitive to such pressures.

A fourth type of motive is found when the planner believes or knows that by committing himself to working for a change he may be able to acquire resources for some other purpose. The resource may be as tangible as funds, buildings, equipment, or personnel. (A social agency may very well commit itself to attempting change in order to attract financial contributions or volunteer manpower.) On the other hand, the resource may be as intangible as prestige. An agency that undertakes a demonstration or pilot project may gain prestige by receiving a grant which can be a symbol of triumph over its competitors, an indication of its competence, a measure of its sincerity, an evidence of its importance.

Planners and their employers rarely commit themselves to attempting a change on the basis of just one motive. The agencies participating in the Ford Foundation projects, committed by terms of the grant to undertaking some efforts at social change, were uniformly impelled by at least two motives. They all wanted to learn from experience and experimentation and they all wished to use the project as a means of gaining further resources.[1] This is not to suggest that they did not have a third motive, a desire to make progress in meeting the needs of their communities.

The mixture of motives which leads a planner to intervene is expressed in his response to situations. If, for example, the planner's dominant motivation is to learn from trying a particular method, he is not likely to respond to crises which deflect him from his experiment. On the other hand, if his predominant motive is to meet certain social welfare needs, then he is not so likely to be rigidly attached to particular styles and methods.

BASIC CHOICES OF APPROACH

Once the general target of change is established through a decision to intervene, a planner determines his basic path or approach to the target. This is a critical choice for it guides most subsequent aspects of the planning sequence.

While the range of alternatives open to the planner is theoretically infinite, it is costly and unnecessary for him to weigh every possibility. The time and money involved in discovering and evaluating every conceivable choice is prohibitive.[2] Instead, relatively satisfactory approaches are considered on the basis of a more limited search.[3] The planner's general sense of cause and effect, acquired through training and experience, serves to limit somewhat the general range from which he will choose.

For many social welfare problems, however, specific knowledge of cause and effect is not adequate enough to narrow fur-

---

[1] See Binstock, "Demonstration-Research in the Planning of Services for the Elderly: an Analysis of Social Agency Project-Sponsorship," in Friedmann and Barkley, eds., *The Uses of Research: a Report on the Applications of Research in Gerontology.*

[2] See Marschak, "Efficient and Viable Organizational Forms," in Haire, ed., *Modern Organizational Theory.*

[3] See Simon, *Models of Man: Social and Rational.*

ther the range to a particular "best" course of action for achieving change. If we limit our attention to the field of aging, we must acknowledge that we are not only uncertain as to the remedies for many problems, but also as to the causes of the problems themselves. Nearly a third of those over sixty-five have significant physical handicaps; perhaps 5 percent live in hospitals or nursing homes. No one can say with much certainty that for any individual a change in diet, whether at age one or age twenty, would spell the difference between health and disability in the sixties. Will annual physical examinations result in better health? Will a particular kind of housing enhance the social life of the aged, or will a network of golden age clubs overcome their loneliness? Will retirement education programs in industry or adult education classes reduce the tension of retirement? Or will an increase in retirement income achieve the same end more effectively? Such uncertainties are not limited to the field of aging. They confound efforts to cope with mental illness, alcoholism, and juvenile delinquency as well.

Despite inadequate knowledge of cause-effect relations, planners do have some guides. There is limited evidence that certain remedies are valuable and have *some* positive effect. What is troublesome is the lack of knowledge about which persons in any population benefit most from one approach as against another. Also, which of several remedies should take priority when they cannot be provided simultaneously? Given the present state of our knowledge as to the origin of social problems and ills, the planner relies, in the last analysis, upon his own axioms—his own mixture of professional training and experience, personal values and beliefs—to choose among the various approaches which seem relevant for solving the problem at hand.[4] The planner's choice of approach will be a cen-

[4] The choice of goals in almost every field of human endeavor is based on a mixture of axioms and calculations. See May, "The Nature of Foreign Policy: the Calculated versus the Axiomatic," *Dædalus*, XCI (1962), 653–67.

tral determinant of the content of his goal—a goal which we have consequently termed a "preference goal."

We have suggested that in contemporary social welfare planning there are three general approaches to meeting needs. One may be termed psychological or "people-changing." [5] The fundamental cause of a person's need is assumed to be his emotional response to the conditions of his life:

It is the environment that is regarded as more static and adjustment is hoped for through the psychological flexibility of the individual, rather than, as earlier, through rendering the environment more amenable to adjustment. This change of focus . . . has affected the technique of individual treatment, for this was concerted into a psychological problem of the client instead of a problem of external adjustment between the individual and social structure.[6]

A man may retire at sixty-five and become disoriented, unhappy, troublesome to friends and family. He may react in this manner because it is difficult for him to accept role change, or because he has a flawed capacity to assess personal relationships and to manage them. Counseling may help him understand more objectively the conditions he faces, his emotional responses, and how to live with his new situation. An anxious patient who risks surgery by refusing to follow a diabetic regimen can be taught by counseling to cope more suitably.

A second approach to the same problems is through a basic change in social systems. This approach sees societal deficiencies as a major cause of individual need. The shock of retirement may be met by amendments to statutes that promote retirement at sixty-five or, perhaps, through the establishment of a national health service.

The same problems might be tackled through a third ap-

[5] See Vinter, "Analysis of Treatment Organizations," *Social Work*, VIII, No. 2 (1963), 4.
[6] Klein, "The Social Theory of Professional Social Work," in Barnes, Becker, and Becker, eds., *Contemporary Social Theory*, p. 766.

proach which assumes that a person's needs can be met by changing an organization's policies. An employer may be persuaded to adopt less rigid employment regulations. Unions may be encouraged to institute classes in retirement preparation. The city health department or a general hospital can be prevailed upon to open health-maintenance clinics. Physicians can be urged by the local medical society to give more attention to the unique problems of their older patients.

Whatever the basic approach selected or preferred by the planner, it is not in itself all that is needed for the development of a goal. What is called for is an explicit statement, as detailed as possible, of what is to be substituted for the unsatisfactory conditions—in short, some operational interpretation of the decision to intervene. It is at this stage that the planner's preferences become embodied in a series of relatively concrete objectives. These objectives inevitably incorporate some interpretation of need and indicate how those needs will be met.

A determination of needs has often proved troubling to planners because they are usually generalists whose attentions are directed at a variety of problems. Rarely are they experts in the details of what is needed in many different fields of professional practice. How, then, shall evidence of needs be procured so that operational plans will have reliable foundations? Whether a planner works alone or as part of a team of specialists, penetrating evidence of need must be accumulated to fill in the details of changes sought, regardless of the preferred basic approach. If the preferred approach in planning for the aging, for example, is to change programs of organizations, he has to find answers to such questions as: Which older persons are adversely affected by present conditions? Where are they located? Which organizations are appropriate for helping them? What program and policy innovations in each organization will be useful—altering the composition, size, or functions of staff;

widening standards of eligibility for service; new patterns of referral? The planner has to gather evidence of need in order to answer such questions.

The traditional method of defining social welfare needs is to draw upon the records and experiences of social welfare agencies. These contain information on caseloads, treatments, requests for help, and demographic data on clients. In essence, this approach redefines need as "demand"—and, at that, the demand of a relatively small and self-selecting portion of a population. Many people do not know about the existence of social agencies and many of those who do, avoid them because they are uncomfortable with programs which are alien to their culture.[7] Agencies also have various devices to limit and control the distribution of their services (families must be residents for a given length of time to be eligible for financial assistance and for health and other services, for example). Moreover, the volume of services is by no means commensurate with the volume or variety of identifiable human needs. Only a small proportion of persons with any need, no matter how objectively measured, is actually known to the current service network. Not more than 25 percent of all persons living below the poverty line (as defined in the Economic Opportunity Program of 1965) are in receipt of financial assistance from a welfare agency.[8] Out of the 50 percent of emotionally handicapped persons who might benefit, only a minor fraction receive therapy.[9] Perhaps 2 percent of the aged receive socially provided care, whereas most estimates suggest that 5 percent or more require it.[10] Despite these limitations, information from agency records is better than no data at all.

Another basic approach to identifying need is a direct survey

[7] Hollingshead and Redlich, Social Class and Mental Illness: a Community Study.
[8] Morgan and others, Income and Welfare in the United States.
[9] Srole and others, Mental Health in the Metropolis.
[10] Taber, Itzin, and Turner, Comparative Analysis of Health and Welfare Service in One County.

of the group of persons to be helped. A much more ambitious undertaking than identifying need through the route of agency "demand," it has the advantage of much more accuracy as a means of identifying the qualities and quantities of needs to be met. While an attempt to interview all persons within a given category poses serious difficulties of locating them and financing the research, it is now possible to secure the same data in an efficient manner through modern sampling techniques.[11] However, few social welfare organizations have been able to undertake such sampling projects; their budgets seldom allow for sizable research operations. One method of overcoming the cost of sampling is to make a secondary analysis of demographic data gathered for other purposes. For example, it is possible to review data as to the income status of persons over sixty-five in a given metropolitan area, the number on public assistance, and the supply and average costs of housing. From this information can be derived some crude estimate of the housing needs of older persons, even though it is a poor substitute for analysis of primary data.

In sum, the planner has certain means with which he can translate his preferred approach into specific combinations of goals which constitute objectives:

1. Evidence of demand from the records of service agencies
2. Judgments of experts
3. Population studies
4. Reanalysis of basic demographic studies

The assessment of need, however, does not in itself enable the planner to develop detailed statements of what is to be done. It does not at all indicate the precise features of a proposed policy change. The specific configuration of alterations for meeting needs must still be chosen.

To make this choice and further reduce the extent to which his

[11] Morgan and others, *op. cit.*, illustrate the methods and advantages of such an approach for a major welfare problem.

goal is a preference derived from axioms, the planner can use fragments of evidence as to the effectiveness of certain measures for meeting need. Let us suppose, for example, that the planner has decided that most of the 2,000 elderly patients in his community suffering from stroke need better care if they are to regain as much as possible of their capacities to function. Let us say that the basic approach he has chosen for meeting these needs is an attempt to change the policies of organizations providing pertinent medical services. He can then examine available data as to the actual effects of various programs of medical care. He can find out, for example, what results have been achieved by certain programs that have provided various arrangements for therapy by professional nurses and by physical therapists, counseling by medical social workers and psychologists, supervision by physicians. The effects of different staff volumes and compositions can be compared. The results of several types of patterns for coordination and referral of cases can be discovered. Such hard data are scarce, but sometimes available. Small-scale demonstrations have established what can be accomplished with various types of therapeutic programs. While information on most programs for meeting needs is fragmentary, if available at all, there are some instances in which it can be used by a planner to enhance the likely efficacy of the specific measure he chooses for improving social conditions. It is one further means through which the planner can introduce an element of rationality into his choice of a solution to the social problems at hand.

The development of preference goals gives the planner an operational view of the tasks that lie ahead. In tracing the development of these goals we have tried to indicate four fundamental sets of choices. The planner must decide to what extent and in what circumstances he is committed to working for change. Second, he must elect his basic approach for coping with social welfare conditions. Third, he must choose his methods for determining need. And fourth, he must specify the details of the changes sought. These choices are refined insofar as possible by objective criteria. But given the nature of such choices, a goal cannot be wholly based upon means-end calculations. Whether the preference goal is actually developed by an individual planner or by his employer, or emerges from the joint deliberations and activities of a planner and his committee, mixtures of rationality and value are involved in the basic decisions. In the last analysis it is a "preference" goal because, regardless of the rational choices that may be included, it is based to some extent upon judgments as to merit.

V · ORGANIZATIONAL RESISTANCE TO PLANNING GOALS

In attempting to achieve a preference goal the planner is immediately confronted by questions of feasibility. When his goal embodies a proposal for a change in the policy of an organization, his success, most simply expressed, lies in his ability to get the "target" organization to accept that proposal. A "policy change" is an innovation in the organization's allocation of its resources. This may include changes in the amount allocated, the combinations allocated, the purposes for which they are allocated, the timetables for allocation, the procedures of allocation, and the criteria for allocation. These changes may affect programs, procedures, activities, and behavior patterns—all the expressions of an organization's purposes as well as the ways in which they are carried out. If the proposed innovations are resisted by the target organization, the feasibility of the planner's goal is determined by his capacity for overcoming that resistance.

For a number of reasons, organizations are predisposed to resist changes embodied in social planning goals. One of the primary reasons is that the "organization does not search for or consider alternatives to the present course of action unless that present course is in some sense 'unsatisfactory.'"[1] The "exist-

[1] March and Simon, *Organizations*, p. 173. For a brief, cogent evaluation of current scholarship on theories of organization and decision-making, and for a bibliography of major pertinent works, see Deutsch and Rieselbach, "Recent Trends in Political Theory and Political Philosophy," *Annals*, CCCLX (1965), 154–55.

ing pattern of behavior has qualities of persistence; it is valuable in some way or it would not be maintained." [2]

Social planning goals are not formulated primarily in an attempt to solve unsatisfactory conditions within a target organization.[3] Rather, major attention is directed toward finding a solution to an unsatisfactory condition of social welfare. Moreover, target organizations are not often selected with attention to the current states of satisfactoriness in their internal affairs. And even if the organization's present course is in some sense unsatisfactory, it is unlikely that the allocative innovation presented by a social planning goal will be perceived by the organization as a solution to its problems. It should not be surprising, then, that preference goals are frequently resisted by target organizations.[4]

Resistance to planning goals has many bases and is expressed in a variety of ways. If an organization is functioning satisfactorily, innovative proposals threaten attachments to old ways, introduce the uncertainties of new practices, and may disrupt the comfortable balance. A change may violate the culture or ethos that provides the foundation for organizational cohesion and financial support. Suggested innovations may appear senseless, insignificant, or without worthwhile purpose. Some alterations may be resisted primarily because they seem to require subordination of the organization to the will of outsiders. Others, of course, are rejected because, in the view of the target organization, the cost of adopting them apparently outweighs the benefits. While any one of these factors may be the most important in a given situation, usually several are opera-

[2] Simon, Smithburg, and Thompson, *Public Administration*, p. 453.
[3] For an explication of the determinants of the criteria of satisfaction see March and Simon, *op. cit.*, pp. 182–83.
[4] To suggest that an organization resists a planning goal is not also to suggest that it is generally resistant to change. As will be suggested further on, an organization may often resist a specific innovative proposal even though it is generally disposed to make a change. *Ibid.*, p. 174.

tive to some degree when organizations resist planning goals,[5] as was evident in the Ford projects.

San Francisco

One of the early undertakings of the San Francisco project director was an attempt to develop a health screening program for the elderly. The proposal called for the establishment of program units in five municipal health clinics, each to be staffed by a physician, a nurse, a social worker, and a health educator. The clinics were to provide case-finding, diagnostic, and educational services; staff members were expected to see to it that patients who needed medical care obtained it from appropriate community facilities.

In developing this proposal, the planner recognized a strong tradition in which voluntary and public health services of San Francisco are compartmentalized. For example, all general medical clinics are administered by voluntary hospitals and supported exclusively by fees and philanthropic contributions. Yet, these private clinics are the sole source of out-patient medical care available to persons with limited incomes who cannot afford private fees. While the city health department administers a public hospital for in-patient care, it is not integrated with any of the private out-patient services. The success of the planner's attempt to establish the health screening program depended upon good working relationships between the private and the public health systems, which in turn required the cooperation of both the San Francisco medical society and the health department.

Both organizations approved the screening plan in principle although the health department indicated that it would make only one, possibly two, of its centers available. While the medical society registered no objections at the outset, it soon became clear that the society would reject any arrangement which implied that existing patterns of private medical practice were in any way inadequate. Proposals for case-finding, diagnosis, and health education services were resisted. ("We're not going to beat the bushes for patients." "There'll be no laying on of hands." "No patients will be disrobed for examinations.") Although the medical society eventually agreed to administer a watered-down version of the program, it refused

[5] See Simon, Smithburg, and Thompson, op. cit., pp. 439–41.

to apply for funds when it learned that a grant from the federal government would probably have to be obtained. ("That's tainted money.")

Another problem tackled by the San Francisco project was the uneven distribution of recreational services for the elderly, provided at the time by some forty social agencies. Despite a plethora of agencies and a variety of auspices, less than 3 percent of the aged population participated in programs with any regularity. Some neighborhoods had no recreational programs at all; where programs existed, participation was often limited to persons of certain ethnic or religious backgrounds. The need for programs serving socially isolated older persons in the downtown rooming-house district was dramatized by a series of well-publicized incidents in which the public library barred them from its reading room and lavatory facilities.

To meet these deficiencies, the planner attempted to persuade various agencies to extend their programs into additional neighborhoods and to acquire more diversified clientele. Both types of proposals were resisted. Some agencies pleaded a lack of funds for program expansion and indicated no willingness actively to seek additional support from any source. Sectarian agencies generally resisted the suggestion that their service responsibility could or should extend beyond their own group.

Contra Costa County

Prior to the inception of the Ford project, the West Contra Costa Council had decided that additional visiting nurse services were needed, and in September, 1961, the project director (planner) was asked to act on this matter. She found that the local Visiting Nurse Association was interested in expanding the range of its program and that other health and welfare agencies had recently called attention to the need for nonmedical home services. A discussion with the county health officer convinced the planner that new nursing and homemaking services should be combined within a single agency, and that such a program would have to be county-wide in order to secure requisite resources. With these premises it became clear to her that cooperation from the county public welfare department was essential for success, and that the participation of certain other organizations would be valuable—the county health department, the county hospital, the heart and cancer associations, and the county medical society. The only likely source for initial funding of the program seemed to be the U. S. Public Health Service.

Several of these organizations expressed immediate reservations, however, when the planner presented her proposal. The county welfare director was reluctant to endorse the program, stating that administrative and legal restrictions prevented him from accepting the proposal that he arrange for the purchase of services from the new voluntary agency, for the benefit of welfare clients. (No doubt the increase in the department's budget which this would entail was a factor, as well as a preference that such services, if introduced, be directly controlled by his department rather than by a new agency.) Other potential participating agencies were inclined to support development of separate nursing and homemaker services. The regional office of the Public Health Service felt that the program as first proposed lacked sufficient innovative character and experimental promise to qualify for a demonstration grant.

Opposition was also encountered within the planner's own organization, the newly established Contra Costa Council of Community Services. The faction from the older, relatively well-developed western region was inclined to oppose the notion of a combined program because it posed a competitive threat to the financial support of the separate nursing and homemaking services already established in that sector of the county. Moreover, the proposal that the new program be county-wide reactivated latent regional antagonisms that had recently been exacerbated when a prominent and aspiring member of the western faction failed to become the executive director of the new county organization.

Another objective of the Contra Costa project director was the construction of low-rent housing for the elderly. When the planner approached the municipal housing authorities in Richmond and San Pablo, cities containing two thirds of the total population of the western region, she found them generally receptive to her aims. However, according to state law, local housing authorities must submit their plans for housing construction to public referenda in their communities. Since the West Contra Costa Board of Realtors had taken a vigorous public stand that no new housing for the elderly was needed, the housing authorities were reluctant to move ahead and thereby expose themselves to the risk of defeat in referenda campaigns.

Other efforts to develop housing for the elderly in unincorporated areas falling within the jurisdiction of the county housing authority found even less responsiveness. After much discussion, the director of the authority agreed to undertake a preliminary survey of need, but he was unimpressed with the urgency of the situation because the proportion of elderly residents was small, their average income was relatively high, and a great deal of middle-income housing had been recently constructed in the county.

Denver

One of the goals of the Denver project was to expand and improve recreational programs for the elderly by bringing about the federation of some thirty-five different clubs of older persons. The programs of these clubs were meagre and sporadic. By consolidating the memberships of many small groups the planner expected to find a fresh demand for a rich and varied program, important enough to require full-time staff supervision and coordination. With this expectation, he sought a commitment of staff from the municipal department of parks and recreation. The department, already operating a day center for the aged, rejected the planner's proposal: any expansion of its program for older citizens would have required diversion of its limited resources from programs for other age groups. The planner also encountered resistance in his attempt to federate the clubs. It soon became evident that club members were relatively satisfied with the pattern of their activities. Perhaps an even more important factor in their reluctance to band together was their obvious fear of losing autonomy.

The Denver project also attempted to develop a program for improving the medical services to chronically ill older persons. His approach was to bring together forty-five health and welfare agencies from the metropolitan area, to get them to agree on the need for better coordination and to develop for themselves new patterns of procedure for interagency relations. While these agencies did participate in a series of meetings and generally agreed that there was some need for coordination, they did not seriously attempt to undertake innovations. They were confounded by a dilemma well stated by the planner as he presented them with two precepts to guide them in their deliberations:

"A program on chronic disease is inherently an all-or-nothing program . . . it cannot be segmented but must reflect integration of services.

"Chronic disease is too big a problem to solve in one fell swoop, and it would be best to start realistically with one aspect of the program and build gradually."

Given this contradiction and the initial participation of forty-five (later sixty) organizations, it is not surprising that this conference group was not able to agree upon a single proposal in the course of three years.

Worcester

The aim of the Worcester project was to establish a center for the elderly which would provide an extensive battery of health and social services. The planner chose two basic approaches as he tried to achieve this goal. One was to seek funds with which to rent facilities and to hire staff; the other was to solicit contributions of staff and space from various organizations in the community.

The primary targets of the planner's search for funds for the multiservice center were the Priorities Committee and the board of directors of the Worcester Planning Council. From the outset there were strong indications that both targets were opposed to the creation of this new agency for the elderly. The Priorities Committee gave the proposed center such a low rating in its periodic evaluation of worthy community causes that the Golden Rule (United) Fund never gave serious consideration to proposals for financial support. Low rating also hampered efforts to secure funds from other likely sources because the decisions of the Priorities Committee as to worthy and unworthy causes are generally respected in Worcester's tightly knit welfare system. After an extended period of frustration for the planner, the Planning Council seemed to relent in its opposition when it granted permission for the project for the aging to undertake independent, local fund raising. But this seeming change of attitude was illusory. Leading figures in the Fund and Council took pains to let important potential contributors know that the multiservice center was not important, and this message was also subtly delivered to a fund-raising specialist who had been ready to manage a campaign for the center on a contingency basis.

Organizations from which the planner was seeking contributions of facilities and staff also resisted his efforts. Several organizations seemed to be promising targets for the contribution of facilities. The YWCA was currently constructing a large modern building in the downtown area, and several of its board members had hinted that the "Y" might be persuaded to let the age center use some available space on the ground floor. But other members of the organization resisted the suggestion on the grounds that "dirty old men hanging around the lobby" might corrupt the morals of the "Y's" young women. The decision of the Priorities Committee reinforced the hesitancy of those who had reservations. Ground-floor space in Worcester's public housing projects also seemed suitable locations for the multiservice center, but the director of the housing authority took the position that housing projects were not appropriate sites for social service programs. For a while it seemed that the Junior League of Worcester would provide volunteer staff for the proposed center program, but effective communications from Fund and Council members led to withdrawal of the offer.

The Worcester project director also tried to alleviate the plight of older persons living in substandard housing in the center of the city. The established practice of the city housing authority was to build "garden" projects in outlying residential areas. The planner proposed the construction of high-rise apartments in the downtown section, suggesting that most older persons already living in that area seemed to prefer the location and benefited from their ready access to nearby health and social service agencies. While the director of the authority had no general objection to housing for the aged, he gave a number of reasons for rejecting the proposals: neither downtown business interests nor the redevelopment authority would allow such potentially valuable sites to be used for tax-exempt purposes; older persons preferred to live in quiet and restful residential areas; automatic high-speed elevators required for high-rise apartment projects would befuddle and frighten aged residents.

DOMINANT FACTIONS IN ORGANIZATIONS

The propensity of organizations to resist innovative proposals embodied in social planning goals poses important practical questions for the planner. Is it possible to predict or anticipate which target organizations are especially likely to resist? How extensively? No classification has yet been developed which provides systematic guidance for predictions as to which organizations, under what circumstances, will resist certain types of planning goals. Further research into organizational behavior may eventually produce refined predictive criteria, but, for the present, social planners must rely upon a sensitive reading of each new situation against an extensive backdrop of relatively intimate knowledge of the pertinent organizations.

While the history of each organization's previous response to various proposals for policy change is helpful, it is at best a very rough guide, since from the viewpoint of the organization the current proposal for change may differ importantly from past ones in ways not readily apparent to the planner, an outsider. Similarly, decision criteria within the organization may alter over time, often in ways so subtle that even key individuals in organizational operations may not have recognized the change. The planner may also be able to read day-to-day clues indicating that an organization considers its situation unsatisfactory in some sense and, consequently, may be predisposed to accept innovations.[6] But the planner cannot really come to grips with the phenomena of organizational resistance by viewing an organization as if it were a single entrepreneur calculating the value of various courses of action. As March and Simon suggest:

[6] As March and Simon have expressed it: "To explain the occasions of innovation is to explain why a program of action that has been regarded as satisfying certain criteria no longer does so." *Op. cit.*, p. 182. March and Simon present a systematic treatment of "the occasions of innovation," pp. 182–86.

Although tangible . . . costs often can be and sometimes are evaluated in monetary terms, it is seldom possible to make accurate estimates of the costs of innovation, and even in situations where it is possible, such estimates are seldom made. Individuals and organizations give preferred treatment to alternatives that represent continuation of present programs over those that represent change. But this preference is not derived by calculating explicitly the costs of innovation or weighing these costs.[7]

The innovative proposal presented by the planner's preference goal is not evaluated by a monolithic organization with a single goal. In complex organizations, many types of roles are performed, each role defined by a different set of constraints, each set of constraints having some effect upon organizational policy. It is safe to say, however, that most innovative proposals presented to an organization are tested against a set of constraints which is widely shared within the organization; moreover, this set has its strongest roots in the major concerns of those persons who are in dominant organizational roles.[8] It is by directing his efforts at the persons who play the dominant roles (not officially, but actually) within the organization that the planner can be most effective in his efforts to overcome resistance. The critical considerations for the planner are who plays the dominant roles in the organization's decision-making, and, in their organizational roles, what are their primary concerns? [9]

Many individuals and groups within an organization may formally participate in decisions or informally affect them, but in any organization certain factions tend to dominate.[10] A sin-

[7] *Ibid.*, p. 173.
[8] Simon, "On the Concept of Organizational Goal," *Administrative Science Quarterly*, IX (1964), 21. It would be fair, of course, to refer to this set of constraints (as Simon does) as organizational goals.
[9] *Ibid.*
[10] Regardless of rules for the acquisition of official power in organizations, designed to achieve and preserve widespread participation in making decisions, the power to make decisions tends to be accumulated in the hands of a few. This is especially true of those organizations committed to mass participation. It was the observation of this tendency in political parties that led Robert Michels to formulate his "iron law of oligarchy." See his *Political Parties*.

gle faction may be in control, or decision-making may be shared among several—a coalition. By and large, four types of factions tend to assume dominant roles within organizations at one time or another: boards of directors; executives; employees; and general membership. While dominant factions differ from one organization to another, it is possible to distinguish the type that dominates in a given organization and to isolate those matters to which it is sensitive. The planner needs information of this kind in selecting his tools for overcoming resistance and deciding how to employ them because the dominant faction is the most promising target for effecting a policy change.

The Board of Directors

Whenever there is a board of directors, it is officially expected to dominate policy in the interests of the organization's constituency. In the case of profit-making concerns, the pertinent interests are those of the owners of the corporation. For voluntary welfare organizations, private universities, hospitals, churches, and other nonprofit, quasi-public organizations, the board performs the functions of guarding and providing for the interests of consumers or clients, consequently, board members are often termed "trustees" or "overseers." The board of a public corporation or agency is expected to make policy "in the public interest." Since the relevant public is the electorate of a given jurisdiction, public directors, frequently designated "commissioners," attain their positions through election, appointment by elected officials, or appointment by administrative officials, such as city managers.[11] In contrast, the incumbent boards of business concerns and quasi-public institu-

---

[11] In the broadest sense, state legislatures and city councils also function, in effect, as boards of directors. Indeed, in the theory of the council-manager form of city government, the city council is regarded as the board of directors of the municipal corporation. See Price, "The Promotion of the City Manager Plan," *Public Opinion Quarterly*, V (1941), 563–78.

tions often play guiding roles in the selection of their successors.

Official distinctions between the major policy matters to be determined by the board and the minor policies that are the responsibility of executives and administrators are frequently quite vague. Directors are expected to control decisions as to the purpose, scope, and character of the organization's activities; administrators are expected to carry out these decisions as efficiently and effectively as possible. In their very nature, of course, decisions as to the purpose, scope, and character of an organization's activities can define the nature of routine operations quite explicitly, especially if the board meets frequently to review administrative activities in the light of broader policy. By the same token, everyday operations can have a significant impact upon over-all policy, particularly if the board seldom meets and does not take an aggressive interest in the affairs of the organization.

Often the board abdicates, or is precluded from performing its expected function. It "rubberstamps" decisions already made, while continuing to perform ceremonial functions. On the other hand, groups much like boards—advisory committees, for example—may not be expected to make policy but often do so in the absence of a strong board or executive.

In a great many organizations, however, the board of directors plays its official, dominant role in policy determination. This is not to suggest that other factions in the organization contribute nothing to policy formation, but merely that, in the last analysis, the board is decisive. Often, a very few members of the board may become the key figures in organizational determinations. The larger the board, the more likely it is that this will happen. On occasion, even a single individual will dominate the board of directors because of his official position (perhaps as chairman), or his personal influence, or the apathy and indifference of the others.

Persons who serve on boards frequently do so for the probable rewards of prestige and sociability:

Among the trustees and directors of universities, hospitals, and welfare organizations . . . the personal prestige which membership provides is often a strong incentive. Board members not only contribute prestige to such boards, but their own prestige is enhanced through association with other high-status community figures and with the institutions themselves.[12]

Board members are thus responsive to activities which enhance the organization's prestige and stature and thereby enhance their own opportunities for recognition.[13] Not all boards, of course, are dominated by such concerns; the boards of some organizations are primarily interested in achieving some ethical or moral goal. Still other boards are comprised of persons who feel obligated to carry on an established pattern of family or group responsibility; these tend to be occupied with the perpetuation of traditions.

It is, of course, important to distinguish between the personal concerns of a board member and those that guide him in his organizational role. While the board member's view of organizational interests is almost always influenced by his own interests, the latter do not fully determine his decisions in an organizational role; nevertheless, organizational considerations rarely conflict with personal ones.[14] It is safe to say that a proposal which violates the personal concerns of board members will be resisted by the organization. By the same token, the

[12] Clark and Wilson, "Incentive Systems: a Theory of Organizations," *Administrative Science Quarterly*, VI (1961), 141.

[13] See Ross and Hendry, *New Understandings of Leadership*.

[14] As Simon has observed: "If we examine the constraint set of an organizational decision-making system, we will generally find that it contains constraints that reflect virtually all the inducements and contributions important to various classes of participants. These constraints tend to remove from consideration possible courses of action that are inimical to survival. They do not, of course, by themselves, often fully determine the course of action." (Simon, *op. cit.*, p. 21.) Also see Clark and Wilson, *op. cit.*, and Barnard, *The Functions of the Executive*.

planner's efforts to overcome organizational resistance will have to be tailored with an eye to these interests.

The Executive

In some organizations, particularly governmental agencies, there is no board of directors. While general policy may be set by legislation or by higher administrative directives, most policy decisions are in the hands of the agency's managing executive. As in the case of board domination, other internal elements may contribute to policy formation, but decisions are dominated by the executive.

In the presence of a board of directors, control may pass to an executive by default. But even if a board is actively exercising its prerogatives, some of the executive's routine functions may enable him to dominate policy. Through the cumulative impact of routine decisions, through the preparation of budgets and agendas, through control of information flow, through his personnel policies, and through his position at the heart of organizational communications he can play a decisive role in policy development.[15]

The primary concerns of the executive differ from those of a board of directors. He is especially interested in the maintenance and enhancement of the organization, in a smooth and efficient performance. Resources must be managed so as to keep his directors, staff, contributors, and consumers relatively satisfied. Since these elements may require different and sometimes conflicting incentives to satisfy them, the executive must see to it that each receives a sufficient supply to hold the organization together.[16] The executive is also desirous of gaining recognition from members of his own organization and from

[15] See Harrell and Weiford, "The City Manager and the Policy Process," *Public Administration Review*, XIX (1959), 103.

[16] See Clark and Wilson, *op. cit.*, where an analysis of incentives that explains organizational behavior from the viewpoint of the executive is presented.

others in his field. The planner's tools for influencing an executive must be selected for their relevance to such matters.

The Staff

Official responsibility for policy decisions is rarely lodged with employees, but they sometimes have an active voice in determining policy. On rare occasions when customary decision-making patterns break down because employee satisfaction has not been sufficiently taken into account, employees may be able to assume a dominant, though temporary, role.[17] Issues of salary, benefits, working conditions, and professional opportunities and ethics may enable a staff to dictate policy in a period of crisis. Such crises are infrequent in social agencies where professional employees are loath to challenge established procedures and regulations, even when they conflict with their assessment of sound professional practice and clients' interests.[18]

While the staff rarely dominates the entire policy range of an organization, professionals in social agencies do tend to have a decisive voice in policy matters directly concerned with client selection.[19] Regardless of official agency policy, their acceptance and rejection of applicants for service inevitably shape the program.

---

[17] See, for example, the report of an experience in Philadelphia by Weiner, "Toward Techniques for Social Change," *Social Work*, VI, No. 2 (1961), 26–35.

[18] See Billingsley, *The Role of the Social Worker in a Child Protective Agency.*

[19] "The social services, which have helped to nourish them, depend to an increasing extent on the valuable skills and specialized knowledge of these occupational groups [the professions]. Because of the contribution they can make, there is a tendency to give these groups more representation upon policy-making and advisory bodies. . . . A possible consequence is that, collectively, more power may come to reside in the hands of these interests." Titmuss, "Social Administration in a Changing Society," in *Essays on the Welfare State.*

Members and Consumers

While the general membership of an organization may periodically select directors or officers to serve as its representatives for determining policy, the candidates are usually part of a predetermined slate composed by incumbent directors. Occasionally, the policies of public agencies are settled by a referendum on a specific question. A few private organizations with a relatively small membership submit issues directly to their constituents.[20] But for the most part the general membership of an organization rarely plays a dominant or even an active role in a policy decision.

Members and consumers (who are in some sense "members" of an organization) may dominate briefly when they are both greatly dissatisfied and sufficiently organized to pose a threat to organizational survival. This usually occurs when their primary interests, the quantity and quality of the organization's product and the ease of their access to it,[21] are grossly neglected. For any given member the criteria for satisfaction may be any among a wide variety of immediate material necessities and states of social and psychic well-being. The subjective character of these criteria [22] makes it difficult for the planner to be guided by an understanding of these concerns in his attempts to overcome organizational resistance.

Opportunities for members and consumers to determine policy are severely limited because they are not usually organized for this purpose. If they are organized, and if the central issue which brings them together is sufficiently strong, they are likely to withdraw to form a separate organization. If the issue

[20] For example, the Family Service Association of America and local units of the YWCA follow this practice.

[21] See, for example, Somers and Somers, *Doctors, Patients, and Health Insurance*, pp. 194–203.

[22] See Banfield, "Does Consumers' Freedom Need Redefining?"

is weak, the opportunity to control policy is short-lived because the coalition will fall apart, lacking sufficient incentive to bind together the otherwise diverse constituent elements.

The relatively distinctive concerns of these various groups that can dominate organizational policy are of critical importance to the planner as he attempts to overcome resistance to the innovation presented by his preference goal. When one faction dominates, it, in effect, is the channel through which the planner must direct his efforts to change policy. The special lenses through which the faction views innovative proposals are the planner's guide to the feasibility of his undertaking.

Whether or not the planner's goal violates the fundamental viability of organizational life, as it is interpreted by board, executive, staff, or membership, determines whether there is a channel open to the planner for overcoming resistance. If the goal is within the range of organizational purpose as interpreted by the dominant group, then that group's special interests are also a guide to the tools which will be needed for overcoming resistance and to where and how they must be employed. Tools which will influence an executive (in line with his preoccupation with organizational maintenance and enhancement and his desire for career recognition) may be quite different from those needed to influence a board of directors (in accordance with its interests in prestige, sociability, and the discharge of traditional obligations). For a planner's goal to be feasible, he must have access to the dominant group and the appropriate means of influencing it. In the rare instances when several factions dominate as a coalition, sharing equally in the power to determine policy, the planner's job is more difficult. Each of the several targets must be attacked if the planner is to overcome resistance. He must possess a wide variety of tools in order to have the necessary chance of success in each channel. And they must be especially powerful because the diversity of primary concerns operative in the policy considerations of such organizations leads to considerable internal conflict in response to innovative proposals. Consequently, it is difficult for coalition-dominated organizations to make any change at all. It is far easier for a planner to overcome the resistance of an organization that is dominated by a single faction.

In some situations it is relatively easy for a planner to know which faction is dominant and to be confident in his assessment of its primary concerns. In San Francisco, for example, the planner knew from his own direct contact with the local medical society that its policy was determined by a board composed of physicians in private practice. While it is not always safe to assume that such a group is primarily interested in maintaining the traditional patterns of medical care in a community, specific evidence was available to buttress this assumption. At that time the medical society was deeply embroiled in a public campaign of opposition to medicare, arguing that the existent system of medical care for the aged was more than adequate. In this light it should have been quite clear from the outset that the Ford project's plan for a health screening program for the elderly, as proposed, would be vigorously opposed by the medical society. The proposal, in itself, clearly implied that the existing system of private medical care in San Francisco was inadequate for meeting the health needs of many older persons. Indeed, it was developed by the planner and his committee because they thought that system to be inadequate.

In this instance, of course, it would have been easy enough to predict the intransigent resistance of the medical society to the planning goal. The organization was not particularly large and complex; it was not difficult to identify the dominant faction. Moreover, its interest in preserving traditional patterns of medical care was well known. However, a planner cannot be expected to be attuned to the factional situation within each complex organization from which he is seeking a policy change; nor can he always be aware of the overriding interests of dominant factions. Considerable study and analysis of factions and interests dominant in various types of organizations will be needed before planners will have sufficient guidance for making reliable predictions as to resistance likely in a variety of situations.

But in the absence of reliable instruments for prediction, attention to factions and their interests is more likely to provide an understanding of a planning situation than an analysis that is built upon an identification of an organization's "functions" and "responsibilities in the community." It is easy enough, of course, to second guess. But it would seem that the extensive waste of time and energy spent by the San Francisco project, in a fruitless attempt to use logic in overcoming the medical society's resistance, could have been predicted. Attention to the dominant interests of the medical society rather than to the logic of its role as "community representative of private physicians," might have suggested more feasible approaches for achieving many if not all of the aims embodied in the health screening program proposal.

Numerous examples can be found in the records of the Ford projects in which attention to similar matters might have led to more feasible and effective planning.

VI · OVERCOMING RESISTANCE
THROUGH INFLUENCE

Given the natural tendency of organizations to reject innovative proposals, a major determinant of planning feasibility is the planner's capacity for overcoming organizational resistance to his goal. If the preference goal is in fundamental conflict with the primary concerns of the organization's dominant faction, it is unfeasible unless it is revised. (The alternatives open to planners in such instances will be discussed in Chapter VII.) But if the goal does not seriously violate the interests of the dominant faction, the latter is still responsive to influence; the goal is resisted, but the planner has opportunities to achieve his preference. In such situations, the feasibility of a planning effort depends upon availability and selection of the appropriate tools for influence. The planner's selection of appropriate resources for influence is not just a matter of his adding up the number of powerful figures and the amount of material resources that stand behind him, assuming that somehow these will influence the target organization and bring about the desired result. It is primarily the character of resources for influence rather than their quantity which is pertinent.

Influence, as previously suggested, is "the ability to get others to act, think, or feel as one intends."[1] "Others" are

[1] It will be recalled that this definition was drawn from Banfield's *Political Influence*. It was selected because it is a relatively simple formulation which, nonetheless, accurately reflects most of the definitions which have been set

those persons who, singly or jointly, dominate the policy determinations of the target organization. The way in which these persons "act, think, or feel" is their response to the planner's proposed policy change. The planner's preference goal—the change he seeks—is what he "intends."

It is meaningless to consider influence without reference to some object. Just as in considering resistance one must ask, "Resistance to what?" it is necessary to establish a context for a discussion of influence by asking, "Influence with whom, with respect to what?" The Priorities Committee of the Worcester Planning Council? The president of the San Francisco medical society? The county director of public welfare in Contra Costa? Or the appropriations committee of a state legislature? To endorse plans for a multiservice center for the aging? To support a proposed program for health screening and referral of elderly persons? To undertake a county-wide program for home medical care? To authorize state grants for support of home care? Answers to questions such as these are necessary if a consideration of influence is to be intelligible, for they indicate which matters are relevant and which are not.

Influence is pertinent to our considerations here, of course, if it is exercised by social planners to overcome an organization's resistance to a proposed change in its policy. We are interested in influence as it affects the dominant faction of a target organization.[2] Moreover, we want to know the extent to which these factions can be influenced to bring about *specific* policy changes. The sphere (scope, area, category) of our considerations is somewhat further defined by attention to policy changes that are proposals for improving conditions of social welfare, that is, preference goals sought by social planners. In short, our interest is in social planning influence.

---

forth by social scientists (see note 14, Chap. I) in recent years. A more abstract formulation can be found in Dahl, "Analysis of Influence."

[2] Our interest extends not only to situations in which these persons can be influenced to perform certain actions, but also to situations in which they can

Various kinds of influence—political, social, economic—are nominally distinguished by an observer in accordance with his primary interest.[3] Those who pay attention to influence because of its effects upon the possession and exercise of governmental authority are interested in "political influence," even though the phenomena under consideration may also be useful in understanding a social planning effort.[4] Conversely, those who pay attention to the impact of influence upon governmental officials because of its relevance to attempts at changing conditions of social welfare are interested in "social planning influence." Regardless of the sphere of interest, however, the basic elements of influence—its nature, its identity, its workings, its sources—are essentially the same.[5] Fundamental, generally agreed-upon concepts set forth in analyses of political influence will be used here for our consideration of planning influence.[6]

---

be influenced not to perform certain actions; in either case, there can be an impact upon organizational policy, which helps to bring about the proposed change. See Banfield, *op. cit.*, p. 309.

[3] The use of an adjective to modify "influence" simply connotes a focus upon the distribution and exercise of influence within a particular kind of sphere or area, or in relation to a particular kind of activity. For example, Dahl expresses his interest in political influence quite explicitly: "For a variety of reasons, the choices made by government officials and enforced by the means available to them are important to many people. We want to know who determines these choices." *Op. cit.*, p. 26. If the interest exists, the same concepts can be used interchangeably to analyze a great many different kinds of influence—certainly, for example, "college influence" and "street-corner influence." Cf. Snow, *The Masters*, and Whyte, *Street Corner Society*.

[4] See Banfield, *op. cit.*, where material previously published as an account of a planning effort is analyzed as a case study in political influence.

[5] While most students of influence are interested in political influence, they do not hesitate to draw examples from other spheres of activity (having little if anything to do with the exercise of governmental power) when setting forth their basic concepts of influence. Dahl writes: "Individuals who have greater than average influence over a given scope are 'leaders.' Thus with respect to their students, teachers are usually but not always leaders; with respect to party nominations, politicians with considerable patronage are generally leaders, etc." *Op. cit.*, pp. 26–27.

[6] In order to avoid a tedious presentation, certain propositions will be set forth without elaboration or citation. Those interested in pursuing a particular point will find it discussed directly or indirectly in Dahl (*ibid.*). General agreement upon certain concepts is referred to in Polsby, *Community Power and Political Theory*, pp. 3–4, where a number of relevant sources are cited.

PATHWAYS OF INFLUENCE

Before examining the various ways in which planning influence works, it is necessary to observe that the exercise of influence seldom can be definitely identified through the observation of any particular case. While a planner may *believe* that a policy was adopted because he has influenced a key figure in an organization, it is difficult to *prove* this beyond doubt. That an organization makes a policy change in a given instance does not establish that it did so in response to influence.[7] Through observation of many cases, it may be possible to establish that a given planner can overcome the resistance of a given organization with respect to certain policy proposals. (Similarly, at a higher level of generalization, it may be ultimately possible to establish that certain types of planners may be able to overcome the resistance of certain types of organizations with respect to certain types of policy proposals.) But on the basis of just a few cases, the exercise of influence can only be imputed or hypothesized. This is not a serious limitation to our present discussion, however, since we are not attempting to document the influence exercised by various planners in specified situations. We merely wish to illustrate the ways in which planning influence works, to enhance understanding of the factors that establish the relative feasibility of a planning endeavor. This, in turn, can provide a foundation for substantial empirical in-

---

[7] As Banfield puts it: "That someone tries to influence a politician and that the politician responds as if he were influenced (perhaps even saying in so many words that he has been influenced) does not prove that he was influenced: he may have intended all along to act as the would-be influencer wanted him to act (perhaps for reasons very different from those of the would-be influencer), and he may have found it convenient to claim that he was influenced. The only way to find out about such things is to get a perfectly honest and straightforward account of his motives from the actor who presumably was influenced. This, of course, is very seldom possible." *Op. cit.*, p. 10. Cf. Dahl, *op. cit.*, p. 32.

vestigation that may establish working guides for effective exercise of influence in various types of planning situations.

How can a planner use influence to overcome an organization's resistance to his preference goal? How does influence get others to act, think, or feel as one intends? Banfield sets forth five distinct ways in which influence works:

(*a*) influence which rests upon a sense of obligation ("authority," "respect"); (*b*) influence which depends upon the wish of the influencee to gratify the influencer ("friendship," "benevolence"); (*c*) influence which works by improving the logic or the information of the influencee ("rational persuasion"); (*d*) influence which works by changing the influencee's perception of the behavior alternatives open to him or his evaluation of them, and which does so otherwise than by rational persuasion (e.g., "selling," "suggestion," "fraud," "deception"); (*e*) influence which works by changing the behavior alternatives objectively open to the influencee, thus either absolutely precluding him from adopting an alternative unacceptable to the influencer ("coercion") or inducing him to select as his preferred (or least objectionable) alternative the one chosen for him by the influencer ("positive or negative inducement").[8]

These elements can be regarded as pathways on which a planner can approach a dominant policy faction in order to overcome organizational resistance. The pathways might be usefully labeled as:

1. Obligation
2. Friendship
3. Rational persuasion
4. Selling
5. Coercion
6. Inducement [9]

[8] Banfield, *op. cit.*, pp. 4–5.
[9] While both coercion and inducement change the behavior alternatives open to an actor, we have listed them as separate pathways because of the distinctions in the character of the action involved, if not in the results.

While each of these pathways can be conceptually and empirically identified as a distinct entity, a planning effort often involves the use of several pathways at once. Inducement, for example, is usually combined with either rational persuasion or selling. The distinctions are valuable, nevertheless, not only because they provide some understanding of the various ways in which influence works, but because they provide a foundation for understanding the alternatives available to a planner for maximum effectiveness in his struggles to achieve a preference goal.

MATCHING RESOURCES AND OPEN PATHWAYS

Although the dominant faction of an organization may be susceptible to influence, it is not necessarily equally susceptible on all pathways. A faction not at all open to rational persuasion or selling, for example, may very well respond to inducement. Consequently, a planner's assessments, in a given situation, as to whether or not a policy faction is responsive to each of the various kinds of influence can critically determine his chances for achieving his goal. His tools, or resources, for planning influence are virtually unlimited. They are any resources, tangible or intangible, which a planner can use to get others to act, think, or feel as he intends. Regardless of his general reservoir of tools or resources and his willingness and readiness to use them in moving down a pathway, his efforts to do so will be of no avail if that pathway is closed. Moreover, even if he has found an open pathway, he needs the tools for influence that match it, appropriate for activating the dominant faction's responsiveness. An influential planner, then, is one who has available a wide variety of tools, enabling him to draw upon the appropriate type for moving down the open pathways to overcome resistance to his preference goal. A list of resources for planning influence would at least include:

1. Money and credit
2. Personal energy
3. Professional knowledge and expertness
4. Popularity, esteem, charisma
5. Social standing
6. Political standing
7. Special position for receiving and controlling flow of information
8. Legitimacy, legality [10]

Most of these resources can be found in the context of organizational life. But while a planner is usually an organizational employee, [11] this does not necessarily mean that these tools are immediately available to him. His professional knowledge and expertness, the personal energy he may be willing to invest in an undertaking, and, occasionally, his popularity or esteem, are usually the only resources possessed by a planner in his own right. Perhaps because these resources are the most easily available and rather easily expended, planners seem frequently inclined to move down the pathway of rational persuasion in their attempts to overcome resistance.

In the Ford Foundation projects the attempts of planners to overcome organizational resistance relied most frequently upon expert knowledge and large investments of personal energy, applied on the pathway of rational persuasion. In almost every instance this pathway was closed, and the planner was unable to influence the dominant policy faction. In San Francisco the planner tried to change the views of the medical society's directors by martialing evidence of the gaps in medical

[10] Compare with a listing of resources for political influence in Polsby, *op. cit.*, pp. 119–20.

[11] To be sure, in the strictest interpretation of our definitions, not all social planners are organizational employees. But those who are not are few. Moreover, those with some professional training are invariably found in a *formal* organizational setting. "Formal" is stressed because most social scientists define organizations in a fashion that reflects Barnard's seminal definition of an organization as a "system of consciously co-ordinated activities or forces of two or more persons" in *The Functions of the Executive,* p. 73.

care received by indigent older persons and of the likely effectiveness of a health screening program in coping with these deficiencies. In an attempt to overcome the resistance of recreation agencies he confronted them with the logic of his proposal for broadening their services.

The Contra Costa planner argued with the director of the county housing authority that some older persons were badly in need of adequate housing, even though the total number of aged in the county was relatively small. She also tried to convince the county welfare director that the medical needs of his aged clients would best be met through a combined program of visiting nurse and homemaker services, offered by a voluntary agency.

The Denver project director tried to persuade representatives of the forty-five organizations participating in the chronic-illness conference group that total coordination of their programs was desirable, regardless of the unwieldy forms it might take. Similarly, he tried to bring about forty senior citizens' clubs into a federation, by arguing that program efficiency could be maximized.

The Worcester planner tried to sway the housing authority director to accept his preference for a downtown project site by pointing to the need of the aged to have access to certain centrally located health and social services, and by emphasizing their desire to remain in the familiar and stimulating environment of their present central-city neighborhood. In attempting to procure an allocation from the United Fund to support a multiservice center, the planner urged that the establishment of this unique, experimental program would attract new funds to Worcester for welfare programs and would provide more efficient service to the elderly.

All these attempts were fruitless. In none of these cases did the target organization accept the planner's preference goal. When dominant factions were approached through rational persuasion, they were not responsive; that pathway was closed. This is not to say that all other pathways were closed; in a few instances a planner was later able to overcome resistance by gathering and using resources appropriate for open pathways of obligation, friendship, selling, coercion, or inducement.

Occasionally, in the Ford projects, the pathway of rational persuasion was open, and the planner's expertness, energy, and esteem were sufficient resources for success. The American Red Cross chapter of Contra Costa was persuaded to organize and administer a program of friendly visiting when the planner suggested that the organization was highly qualified and experienced for such an endeavor and was likely to enhance its standing in the welfare community by undertaking it. The Worcester project director influenced a bank to grant or withhold loans to nursing homes on the basis of the quality of their services. He argued that homes that provided a high quality of services were likely to be more profitable and thus better credit risks.

The cluster of resources immediately possessed by the planner usually proves to be inadequate for overcoming organizational resistance. Expertness, energy, and esteem are useful for influencing policy-making factions which are open to rational persuasion and selling. But these pathways are frequently closed; martialing of facts and intensification of energies are not likely to open them. It is this kind of mismatch of pathways and tools for influence that so often frustrates social planners. They have appropriate resources for moving down the pathways that are closed; they lack resources for moving down the pathways that are open.

In rare instances, expertness, energy, and esteem conceivably could be useful on other pathways than those of rational persuasion and selling. Assuming, for example, that the pathway of obligation is open, it is possible to imagine a situation in which the planner's professional competence might engender a sufficient sense of respect or authority to be useful to him in overcoming resistance. Similarly, it is possible to imagine instances in which expertness could be used as a resource for influencing through friendship, coercion, and inducement. But in our review of the Ford projects and similar planning activities we find little if any indication that expertness was or could have been used effectively on these other pathways. In the type of social planning considered here, expertness (and energy and esteem as well) seems primarily (if not exclusively) effective on the pathways of rational persuasion and selling.

In considering some of the other resources for influence used in the Ford projects, the same kind of picture emerges. Each resource seems exceptionally well-suited for use on some pathways, but rarely suited for use on others. Money and credit are especially appropriate for coercion and inducement. Social standing seems to be geared to influencing through obligation and friendship. Political standing seems fitted for use on the pathways of obligation, coercion, and inducement. A special position for receiving and controlling flow of information seems best adapted for selling. And legitimacy and legality are most suited for use on the pathways of obligation, coercion, and inducement.

Resources appropriate for open pathways can often be acquired through exhaustive searching and skillful development. These tools for influence can sometimes be found within the organization that employs the planner, but they are not necessarily at his disposal. While most such organizations have their own material resources, they are rarely uncommitted and available for use by the planner. They frequently have a pool of more or less influential members with social and political standing who control jobs and credit, or are respected for their wisdom and judgment. Yet it is not at all certain that they will support attempts to achieve any specific preference goal. Some of these organizations are sufficiently respected in civic affairs to be able to legitimize a welfare undertaking; this capacity, however, is not controlled by the planner.

The Ford Foundation projects clearly demonstrated how uncertain is the availability of resources within the planner's own organization, and how difficult it is for him to draw effectively upon them. Time after time the planner was unable to get hold of them for his purposes; even when he could, he often found that they were not, in fact, useful resources for influence at all. In general, it is safe to assume that persons with social and political standing are resources for exercising influence; but in specific instances they may have little or no influence.[12]

In Worcester the planner was employed by the Planning Council, which provided the recommendations relied upon by the Golden Rule Fund in raising and allocating money for social welfare programs. The planner sought the aid of his colleagues in influencing the Council's Priorities Committee so that, ultimately, the Fund's resistance to his proposal for a multiservice center for the aging could be overcome. Despite his intensive efforts, however, they would not provide strong support for his case, and the committee refused to rank the center project high enough to make possible an allocation from the Fund.

A different type of disappointment in securing the use of an organizational resource was encountered in San Francisco. The project director was concerned about the relatively low standards of social service provided by the department of welfare. When the planner proposed that the department offer additional casework services for the aged, the welfare director

---

[12] In the strictest sense, money, political and social standing, and other resources cannot truly be regarded as resources for influence until they have actually been effective in a concrete act of influence. In other words, they are not resources except in the past tense. As Dahl has observed: "The idea of potential influence, which seems transparently clear, proves on examination to be one of the most troublesome topics in social theory." Dahl goes on to present an imaginary dialogue between A. and B., two observers in New Haven, which brings out some of the troublesome aspects of analyzing potential influence. *Who Governs?* pp. 271–73.

objected to the implication that his program was inadequate. He asserted that the needs of his department's elderly clients were relatively small when compared to the needs of 80,000 other older persons. Moreover, he was determined to maintain a record which would permit him to show unexpended departmental appropriations for each fiscal year. The planner's attempts to overcome the director's resistance with logical arguments were of no avail. One of the active members of the Social Planning Committee of the United Community Fund (the planner's employer) was a descendant of an early San Francisco family, well-placed socially, and with great influence in philanthropic circles. Since he was also chairman of the public welfare commission, to which the director of public welfare is accountable, he seemed a natural resource for influence in this instance. Initially, he was reluctant to have any role in supporting the planner's aim. The planner eventually persuaded him that he bore a special responsibility to use his influence and authority, and he tried to do all he could to change the welfare department's policy. It soon became evident, however, that he had very little influence for getting this particular preference goal accepted. Indeed, it may have been this fruitless effort that led the mayor to pass him by a few months later when his term on the welfare board expired, and he was not reappointed.

In the last analysis, the extent to which a planner can rely on the resources of his own organization depends upon the degree to which those in it share his determination to achieve a given preference goal, and the extent to which their apparent general influence is effective for the specific purpose at hand.[13] The planner can also find, of course, many appropriate and useful resources outside his own organization. Material resources can be secured from state and federal agencies, private founda-

[13] See Binstock, "Determination, Equipment, and Strategic Position"; Randall and Morris, "Planning and Organization of Community Services for the Elderly," *Social Work*, X, No. 1 (1965), 96–102.

tions, and individual contributors. Influential citizens who are not members of his agency may be receptive to his pleas for support. Expert knowledge and guidance can be obtained from universities and other organizations. While these possibilities are virtually unlimited, it is extremely difficult to convert them into resources for influencing the target organization. Each of these persons and organizations has previous commitments and responds to approaches for aid in relatively distinctive fashions. Few planners have sufficient experience and information to be able to select out and unlock the right resource at the right time from among all these possibilities.

The funds required for the proposed health screening program in San Francisco were not available from either the planner's own organization or the target organizations. In an attempt to make her goal feasible she sought financial support from governmental agencies and a private foundation. The U.S. Public Health Service was eager to make demonstration grants for experimental medical programs for the elderly, but its views and the views of the San Francisco planner as to what was sufficiently experimental were widely divergent. A private foundation was generally interested in supporting new welfare services, but after much exploration and investigation proved to be indifferent to health projects.

To achieve many of the goals in the Contra Costa project, the planner thought it necessary to have the support of influential persons. Since her own organization, newly formed, lacked a reservoir of strong leadership, much of her energy and effort was devoted to locating individuals who might be useful for this purpose, and persuading them to join her organization and exert themselves on behalf of her preference goals. While she was able to find a number of persons who were only too happy to be appointed as directors of the Council and as committee officers, they proved to be reluctant to support her goals vigorously and continuously. The planner recruited as chair-

man of her committee a high-level executive of a leading
nationwide industrial firm who had many years of experience
as a leader in civic and social welfare activities. But he shortly
proved to be more or less indifferent to projects for the elderly.

On occasion, the planner's own organization makes it difficult for him to obtain outside resources because the possibility
of his success threatens comfortable patterns, procedures, and
positions. In searching for a place to locate the multiservice
center for the aging, the Worcester planner found that the
local Salvation Army was glad to make space available. However, the planner's own organization considered this resource
to be unsuitable even though the space offered was, in itself,
desirable. It felt that the image of the Salvation Army in
Worcester would diminish community regard for the center program. For similar reasons the planner was prevented from making use of several other offered locations which, for the immediate purposes of the program, were quite appropriate.

The ability to control appropriate and effective resources for
influence is essential to a planner's success. And yet, his capacity to do so is severely limited. His resources of expertness,
energy, and esteem are often ineffective because the pathways
of rational persuasion and selling, for which they are most
fitted, are frequently closed. Resources suitable for use on open
pathways can be found within the planner's own organization
and in many other locations. But their availability to the
planner for his purposes can hardly be assumed. It is difficult
to judge which of the resources that seem generally available
can be obtained for a specific undertaking. Moreover, even if
they can be obtained, they may not prove to be resources at all
for overcoming the resistance of a target organization to a certain proposal. It is these difficulties that so often account for
the unfeasibility of planning efforts which, when initially
undertaken, seemed quite feasible.

Even when a planner's capacity to exercise influence effectively is severely limited, however, he still has some alternatives which can help him to achieve much of that which he, or those for whom he is acting, values in his preference goal. A planner with inadequate power or influence is able to apply some technical skills that can enable him to carry forward a feasible planning effort. His preference goal may be unfeasible because he is not able to exercise the right kind of influence for overcoming organizational resistance. But a close analysis of the relations between resistance and influence can illuminate a number of promising courses of action still available to him.

VII · EVALUATING THE FEASIBILITY OF GOALS

We began our consideration of organizational resistance and planning influence as if the relationships between the two were essentially quantitative. It should be clear by now, however, that it is possible to visualize resistance-influence relations in a way that more adequately reflects the complexities of feasible planning. Resistant organizations may be totally unresponsive to influence, responsive to all types of influence, or responsive to one kind of influence (on one pathway) but not another. There are a number of ways in which influence works. Some of the many resources or tools for influence are suitable for use on certain pathways but not on others. And, in many instances, just a few limited resources are immediately available to, or obtainable by, a planner.

A comprehension of the relations among all these variables helps to clarify the available alternatives as a planner attempts to achieve his goal within the inevitable confines of feasibility. The full merits of a preference goal, as envisioned by the planner or by those who have employed him to work for its fulfillment, may not be possible to attain. But a full and conscious understanding of factors that determine the relative feasibility of the situation posed by an attempt to achieve that goal can help even a planner who possesses negligible influence to realize the full potential from his efforts (if, of course, he is not constrained by his employer from certain decisions and actions). Reliable distinctions can be made between unfeasible and feasible goals, and resources can be conserved and employed accordingly. Moreover, it is possible to separate the hopelessly unfeasible goals from those that can be rendered feasible by competent decisions and actions. A recognition that his goal is unfeasible should not necessarily preclude a planner from continuing his attempts, for there are two general courses of action which are available for making his efforts feasible. On the one hand, under certain circumstances he may be able to gain control of appropriate resources for moving down an open pathway to the dominant faction of the target organization. On the other hand, resources already available can be brought into play effectively if he can open up a pathway that was previously closed. The various alternatives can be most clearly seen by examining the elements in three basic types of situations.

UNFEASIBLE GOALS

Unsuitable Planning Preferences

When a planner's preference goal violates the primary concerns of the target organization's dominant faction, all pathways of influence are blocked. The dominant faction is totally unresponsive to influence. The planner's application of any kind of resources for overcoming resistance will be fruitless. A "violation," in this sense, is more than an infringement of specific interests and views. A preference goal that violates the primary concerns of an organizations's dominant faction embodies a policy change which, if instituted, would upset the fundamental material, social, cultural, ethical, operational, and other principles that are the basis of organizational viability. All efforts to achieve such a goal in its current form will be wasteful and ultimately unsuccessful. Since the pathways of influence are closed, no accumulation of additional resources will make it possible to overcome resistance. If the planner wishes to persist in his attempt to improve conditions of social welfare by changing the policy of this target organization, he must alter the nature of the innovation he seeks.

Since the planner must open up a pathway of influence by making his goal more in harmony with the basic concerns of the policy faction, it will not be useful simply to scale down the size of the change that is sought. However, it may be possible to eliminate the sense of violation by *substituting* an entirely different type of innovation. A goal revised in this fashion may not be resisted at all, but even if it is, some pathways of influence may now be open for overcoming the organization's resistance.

For example, the San Francisco planner's desire to see that older persons in downtown rooming houses could have ready access to the social services they needed, was initially embodied in a goal which proposed that several agencies organize a combined central referral office to assume responsibility for procuring appropriate services for tenants in the area. This posed a threat to the autonomy of the agencies in setting eligibility and admission standards, because their decisions were to be subordinated to those of the proposed central office. When this preference goal was resisted, the planner revised it by proposing that these same agencies join in a series of case conferences, to describe their respective admission and service programs and to work for effective, though informal, coordination. This proposal for coping with the initial social problem was accepted by the target agencies.

Another possible response to an unfeasible situation is to *redirect* the initial preference goal to another suitable target organization which may not find the proposed innovations so repugnant. When the Worcester housing authority was totally unresponsive to the planner's attempts to get a multiservice center for the aging located in a public housing project, he shifted his sights. He found the YWCA to be a promising target for the same goal. Although the "Y" offered some resistance, the planner was ultimately able to find an open pathway through which he could successfully exercise influence.

An ever present risk in redirecting or substituting for an unsuitable preference goal is the natural tendency to be overly discouraged by initial rejections. A hasty decision to redirect efforts toward one organization that is almost certain to respond favorably often leads a planner to overlook other less obvious and more difficult targets which offer feasible opportunities for more important policy changes. The risk is particularly pronounced when the planner keeps the same target organization but substitutes a different type of innovative proposal. In his desire to present a policy change that is more consonant with the dominant faction's primary concerns, a planner frequently selects a goal which, if fulfilled, will bring about little if anything in the way of important innovations. As the substitute goal is developed, more attention is given to accommodating the target organization than to bringing about social change.

The substitution made by the San Francisco planner provides a fairly representative example. The proposal for a series of informational conferences among casework agencies (substituted for the goal of a central referral office) was accepted. But the achievement of this goal was negligible as a step toward making social services accessible to older persons in the downtown district. It was this accessibility, after all, which was the valued aspect of the initial preference goal. A more considered reaction to the target agencies' resistance might have yielded a substitute that offered more of an opportunity to attain this central objective. When the agencies rejected the proposal for a joint referral office, the planner might have asked one of them to assume this responsibility, regardless of jurisdictional hassles likely to ensue as it referred each case for service. Such a proposal would offer no threat to the autonomy of this one target agency (as the initial preference goal had done). On the contrary, the enhancement of the agency's prestige and authority likely to accrue from performance of this function might well induce it to respond favorably, and lead to at least some improvement in the accessibility of social services. It is far easier to speculate retrospectively as to what might have been done than to confront the problem in practice and find a useful solution applicable to the immediate situation. But attention to the variables that make for feasibility helps to clarify alternatives for maximizing planning achievements.

Unsuitable Resources

A goal that is unfeasible because of a mismatch of resources and pathways presents the planner with additional opportunities to make decisions which can enable him to carry forward his planning effort. When the primary concerns of the policy group are not violated by the preference goal, one or more pathways for influence may be open, providing the planner with opportunities for overcoming resistance. In this kind of situation, however, the planner is often unable to take advantage of his opportunities because he lacks the appropriate resources. The pathways of obligation, coercion, and inducement may be open, for example, and the planner may possess expertness, energy, and esteem as resources for influence. Nevertheless (assuming that all other pathways are closed), he will not be able to overcome the organization's resistance because these resources are not suitable for use on those pathways, despite the fact that they are open. If the planner wishes to continue trying to achieve his preference goal, he must either open up a pathway suited to his resources, or acquire resources which can be exercised along the pathways already open.

The options of substitution and redirection are still useful in this type of situation. But here, by simply altering the scale of his preference goal, the planner may be able to achieve feasibility without changing the basic character of the policy innovation sought or directing his efforts toward a new target. By increasing or reducing the size or scope of the initial innovation sought from the target organization, he may be able to open up a pathway that was previously closed or obtain new resources. Reduction in the scale of a goal is probably the most obvious adjustment for eliciting responsiveness from a target organization. Increases in scale, which can be equally effective for this purpose, are rarely considered as alternatives by social planners. Perhaps it is because of this neglect that goal adjustments to attain feasibility have so often been regarded as sins of accommodation which compromise the integrity of planners.[1]

Pathways of influence are often closed because the target organization is indifferent to the planner's proposal. The policy faction does not explicitly reject the goal, but does not find it sufficiently significant to be worthy of serious attention. An increase in the size of a proposal may convert it into a possible solution for a social problem of pressing importance and, thereby, attract favorable interest from the target organization. Even if the goal is not intrinsically interesting to the policy faction as a social welfare measure, its transformation into a major undertaking which captures the interest of other parties in the community may make it difficult for the organization to remain indifferent.

The struggle in Worcester to establish a multiservice center for the aging resulted from an earlier attempt to convert a demonstration, part-time information service, manned by volunteer staff, into a full-time, permanent operation. The Community Services planning council took no action on the planner's request that it endorse this proposed operation as a worthwhile community program. He then increased the scale

---

[1] See Morris, ed., *Centrally Planned Change*, pp. 29–40.

of his goal by suggesting that several health and social service functions be added to the information service. This larger objective was also resisted at first, but when it became apparent that the multiservice center proposal had attracted favorable attention from a grant program of the U.S. Public Health Service, the council's endorsement was secured.

Retrospective consideration suggests a number of instances in the Ford projects in which an increase in the scale of a preference goal might have led to concrete achievements. In Denver, for example, the attempt to launch a home-care program for chronically ill older persons was unsuccessful. The target agencies expressed no strong resistance or hostility to the planner's proposal; they seemed to be open to inducement and rational persuasion. But the planner, with few resources useful for inducement, and lacking expert knowledge as to the organization and delivery of medical care, largely relied upon the initiative of the target agencies for development of a program. An increase in the scale of this goal, however, might very well have made available resources suitable for the open pathways. The planner could have developed the modest initial goal into a major proposal for a large-scale program to cope with chronic illness among homebound older persons in Denver, with elaborate specification of details for staffing, financing, and coordination of operative responsibility to be assumed by local health and social service agencies. A bold proposal of this sort would have quite likely attracted strong support from governmental officials and professional experts, thus making it possible to acquire funds and prestige for use as inducements. Moreover, the knowledge of these experts might have proved useful as resources for rational persuasion.

This kind of speculation as to a possible course of action relies upon a series of conditional assumptions, and is easy enough to put forth after the fact. Perhaps in Denver, at the time, some link in this hypothetical chain of "ifs" would have

been impossible to forge. But a planner guided by some understanding of the elements that make for feasibility is in a position to find many such alternatives for achieving concrete results, by matching open pathways with appropriate resources.
In one instance, for example, the Denver planner was skillful in
acquiring an effective resource by revising his preference goal.
He was trying to coordinate the program of the independent
Senior Citizens' Council (SCC) with that of the Metropolitan
Council for Community Service (MCCS). The dominant chairman of the SCC resisted proposals for coordination because his
organization was expected to play a role subordinate to that of
the MCCS. For many months the planner used a number of
resources—logic, the prestige of MCCS board members, and
others—in an unsuccessful attempt to overcome the chairman's
resistance. Finally he revised his goal; instead of seeking a
coordinative arrangement he proposed a merger, and thereby
secured a resource for overcoming the SCC's resistance. The
design for a merger created a new position in the MCCS, a
prestigious appointment which was a sufficient inducement to
bring about the SCC's chairman's cooperation. It also gave him
access to the MCCS resources for his purposes.

A decrease in the scale of a goal is a familiar choice of planners. Resistance is often encountered because the policy faction feels that the planner is "asking for too much." The
proposal is regarded as presumptuous or far beyond the capacity of the target organization's resources. If the planner reduces
his proposal to what the policy group considers "reasonable
proportions," new pathways for influence may be open or resistance may even be eliminated. A typical example was the
experience of the San Francisco planner when he attempted to
establish a health screening program. When the city health department balked at providing facilities for five screening centers, the planner suggested that one or two might suffice. This
compromise was accepted.

A drastic reduction of a goal in order to make it feasible may often lead, however, to total elimination of the valued aspects of the preference goal. When the San Francisco medical society resisted proposals for aggressive case-finding procedures and comprehensive physical examinations in the health screening program, the planner eliminated these features, whereupon he was able to persuade the society to approve the program. This, in effect, was an abandonment of the endeavor to bring about change, because without the case-finding and the examinations the program would provide virtually nothing in the way of health service. In a case of this kind, reduction is not an effective alternative for achieving results. The San Francisco planner might have been better advised to undertake a different type of revision, perhaps a redirection in which the public health department might have been asked to assume total responsibility for the health screening operation.

A planner does not necessarily need to revise his preference goal in order to make his planning effort feasible. An alternative is to accumulate resources for influence. But it is difficult to acquire resources, because of the many difficulties discussed in the previous chapter. Moreover, even when a planner can overcome these difficulties and obtain certain resources, they will be ineffective unless they are appropriate for use on an open pathway. However, the failure of an acquired resource to have the desired result does not necessarily indicate that the pathway on which it was used was closed or that the same resource would not be effective on other pathways. Rather, the lack of success is often due to the unsuitability of the resource for the particular open pathway.

The Worcester planner, for example, was able to bring in a top executive of a major national manufacturing concern and a nationally respected expert in gerontology and have them try to persuade board members and staff of the Planning Council and the Golden Rule Fund that the multiservice center would be worthwhile. They had little effect, for these organizations were not open to rational persuasion. But the Council and Fund were, apparently, open to inducement because when they learned that the U.S. Public Health Service was interested in providing funds for the center, they were only too happy to endorse the project.

In San Francisco the planner tried to persuade the director of the California department of finance to rescind a proposed reduction in payments to nursing homes for public assistance patients because the reduction would make it difficult for the homes to improve their services. The planner's arguments had no effect, but the department later changed its policy after much agitation by, and pressure from, the San Francisco Central Labor Union, a hospital administrator, directors of several municipal welfare departments, nursing home operators, and friends of the governor.

Much of a planner's time and energy is devoted to the accumulation of resources, yet so little of this is ever translated into achievement of even a portion of planning goals. An examination of the Ford Foundation projects suggests that much of this waste might have been avoided and many unsuccessful proposals rescued if the planners had been able to make considered decisions as to which types of resources could be effective, *before* they undertook general efforts to accumulate resources without attention to their suitability for the purposes at hand. There is little evidence, in most instances, that they thought through possibilities for making more effective matches between resources and open pathways for influence. Consequently, there was much waste. The Worcester planner, for example, was eventually able to find resources appropriate for the open pathway of inducement. When he was able to obtain grants from state and federal health agencies, they served as effective resources for inducement, and resistance of both the Council and the Fund was overcome. But in the meantime

many immediately available resources and laboriously acquired ones, unsuitable for use as inducements, had been fruitlessly expended.

FEASIBLE GOALS

When there is a feasible goal, a pathway to the policy faction is open, and the planner has the right resources with which
to move down it, to influence the dominant group, and to overcome the target organization's resistance. All that is needed is
one pathway and resources to match it. While such a goal is
feasible, success is not guaranteed. The planner is in a position
to achieve his goal, but whether or not he does depends upon
his skill in management of resources as he negotiates the pathway (see Chapter VIII).

A readily feasible planning situation is not always easy to detect. A failure to make this identification can be costly. A feasible situation may exist when a planner has only a single type of
useful resource, when he possesses additional types as well, or
when promising opportunities for the acquisition of other
resources are evident. Any attempt to do more than apply the
appropriate type of resource is wasteful. An expenditure of
available but inappropriate resources will do nothing to increase the chances of success; they can be conserved for use in
achieving other goals. Similarly, wasting time and energy in
acquiring additional resources delays action; they can be better
used for other planning efforts. The Denver planner, for example, sought to establish a permanent conference group of nonprofit homes for the elderly, as a means for assuring coordination of their programs. The homes immediately responded to
his proposal, came together, and established a permanent
framework for continued meetings. While there were no indications that this arrangement would atrophy if the participants
were left alone, the planner invested a great deal of his expert-

ness and energy in providing service to the proprietors of each of the homes: compiling brochures about their programs to help the homes attract residents; obtaining information about legislation and tax benefits. These services in no way seemed to affect the already manifest willingness of the group to continue coordination of their efforts. Similarly, the Worcester planner spent much time pursuing a variety of possible contributors of space for the multiservice center: the Salvation Army, the park department, and the public housing authority. Yet the YWCA was the first possibility to come to his attention, and it ultimately provided the location for the center.

LIMITATIONS IN COMPREHENDING FEASIBILITY

A planner inevitably makes a judgment as to the feasibility of his preference goal. Sometimes this judgment is implicit, providing a foundation for a swift transition from the stage of goal and target selection to the stage of implementing action. At other times it may be quite explicit, made with studied reference to the indices of resistance and influence which we have considered. Regardless of the manner in which this judgment is made, it is in response to one of the three types of feasibility situations outlined above. This decision is unavoidable in any kind of planned effort to achieve innovative goals. As March and Simon have observed in considering internal administrative innovations:

At each stage of the process, a feasibility judgment must be made: a judgment that when the time comes to specify the program in greater detail at a later stage, it will in fact be possible to discover such a detailed program. If it later turns out that this judgment was incorrect—no such program can be found—then it is necessary to return to a higher level of the means-end hierarchy and review that part of the process.[2]

[2] March and Simon, *Organizations,* p. 191.

The complex relationship between resistance and influence can be understood in retrospect in the terms which we have outlined. Yet it is a far different matter to suggest that this perspective is useful to planners in their day-to-day efforts. (Moreover, the constraints of a planner's employment situation may preclude him from pursuing courses of action that he deems desirable.) Even if planners attempt carefully to evaluate the feasibility of their undertakings by considering which pathways are open and which resources can be used on them, they cannot be expected to predict the situations with any accuracy. The answers to far too many questions are lacking.

Too little is known about which types of organizations are most likely to resist which types of policy changes. What factions tend to dominate policy in what kinds of agencies? What is the difference between public and private organizations in this respect? Between religious and nonsectarian agencies? Between profit-making and nonprofit concerns? Moreover, what are the primary interests of characteristic types of dominant factions? Are there kinds of influence to which each is most and least responsive? Against what criteria does each type of faction test proposals for allocative innovations? Answers to these questions and others are needed if we are to understand how various types of organizations perceive the costs and benefits of accepting various types of proposals for change.

At the same time it is necessary to distinguish among the kinds of change sought from organizations. What kind of change in an organization's policy—in purpose, program, procedures, or activity—is most likely to bring about the improvement in social welfare which the planner seeks? Which of these is most and which is least likely to be resisted by any given type of organization?

For given types of changes sought from given types of organizations, what types of potential resources actually prove effective for exercising influence? Are expertness and knowledge sufficient for persuading a sectarian organization jointly to sponsor a program with agencies of other sects? Can prestige and social standing be effective resources for inducing the local United Fund to allocate money for a new agency to serve the elderly? Under what circumstances?

Firm answers to these and similar questions may not be easily forthcoming, but it is certainly possible to establish through research some useful indicators for predicting the dominant faction in a given organization, its concerns, its reaction to a given proposal, the pathways on which it will be open to influence, and what appropriate resources will be available. The lack of such answers and indicators has not only placed limits on our capacity to comprehend feasibility and the planning process, it has also resulted in an extraordinary waste of human and material resources committed to improving conditions of social welfare.

If prediction is handicapped by the meager state of present knowledge, a conceptual understanding of the factors that make for feasibility can be of immediate practical value. As we have tried to indicate with our brief applications of hindsight to examples from the Ford projects, a full, conscious consideration of the relations between goals, resistance, and influence can often indicate promising courses of action. A careful attempt to match resources to open pathways not only can help to avoid waste, but can often aid a planner to achieve maximum results from his planning efforts.

THE EFFECTS OF LIMITED COMPREHENSION

The many goals of four Ford Foundation projects were summarized in Chapter III. What was achieved in these communities over three years' time? [3] Those measurable accomplish-

---

[3] The experiences in three other Ford Foundation demonstration projects, not reported in this volume, were similar in all major respects to the four discussed here.

ments which can be traced directly to the efforts of the projects at the time of their conclusion were:

San Francisco

1. The Red Cross chapters trained and organized from 80 to 100 volunteers for friendly visiting.
2. An inventory of senior citizen centers was published.
3. A threatened reduction in nursing home reimbursements was forestalled.
4. The department of welfare and the Family Service Association participated in a national demonstration program for training staff in meeting the needs of the elderly.
5. Communication was strengthened between the San Francisco Information Service and the directors of social agencies.
6. Promising prospects were developed for establishment of a program in employment training for older workers.

Contra Costa

1. A county program of homemaker and home nursing services was established.
2. The Red Cross chapter initiated a friendly visiting service.
3. One hundred and forty new units of low-cost housing for the elderly were constructed.
4. Three drop-in recreation centers were opened.
5. A strong county-wide committee for planning for the aged was created.
6. One specialist in working with the elderly was added to the West Contra Costa office of the state employment office.
7. A cooperative program for social services was launched by the Pittsburg housing authority and the county welfare department.

Denver

1. Two groups were established to consider coordination of health services and nonprofit homes for the aged. The first of

these sponsored a referral service for the chronically ill.

2. Two organizations concerned with planning for the elderly merged.
3. The Family and Children's Service employed one caseworker to concentrate on needs of the elderly.
4. The municipal recreation department allocated additional staff time for senior club programs.
5. The adult education association undertook a small program of preretirement education.
6. A general hospital started a private home medical care program after widespread urging in which the project on aging shared.

Worcester

1. A new agency was established to provide multiple services for the elderly.
2. Approximately forty units of low-cost public housing for the elderly were constructed in the downtown location desired by the project.
3. Recreational therapy was provided one day a week throughout a full year in each of five nursing homes.
4. The Family Service Association assigned one caseworker to the special needs of the elderly.
5. A bank adopted a new loan policy, designed to encourage improvement of services in commercial nursing homes.
6. Several senior citizens' clubs were persuaded to visit older patients in state hospitals and nursing homes.

Other less concrete achievements might be claimed. No doubt, some individuals in the various communities are now more sensitive to the needs of the elderly and more predisposed to support efforts on behalf of the aged. But the eventual meaning of such changes is problematic. Perhaps some agencies which did not change their policies may be more ready to do so the next time they are approached.

While there is no way of actually totaling what was expended to achieve these results, it is clear that an enormous amount of material and human resources was invested. The Ford Foundation provided more than $200,000. The local sponsoring organizations contributed office space, telephone service, secretarial help, office supplies, and the part-time services of a dozen professional employees, as well as their auspices. Several hundred laymen served on numerous committees and undertook many missions on behalf of planning goals; in San Francisco alone, more than 250 persons served on 30 committees, some meeting weekly. The effectiveness of some of these laymen in social welfare causes was considerably diminished because they were used in situations where their stores of good will and influence were expended in unfeasible causes. The staffs and policy factions of more than a hundred local organizations were involved in extensive negotiations which, far more often than not, had no lasting result. The staffs of several national agencies, both private and governmental, were involved in field trips, conferences, correspondence, and negotiations.

There are no rigorous scientific criteria for measuring the results achieved from this expenditure. But it is possible to apply some standards for evaluation. First, the concrete achievements can be compared with the project goals set forth in Chapter III. Certainly it can be said that a relatively small proportion of the goals was achieved. This could, of course, be attributed to "overly ambitious planning." One can argue that the small ratio of achievements to goals is simply due to "unrealistic optimism" in attempting to attain so many objectives. On the other hand, a second, rather subjective criterion also yields a picture of quite limited accomplishment. If the total expenditure in human and material resources is placed alongside the list of achievements, one cannot escape a feeling of disproportion. A great deal of effort seems to have produced very few results. Professional talent and material resources are too scarce, and the time and support of influential laymen too valuable, for anyone at all concerned with the urgent need to cope with conditions affecting the elderly to feel that these results are satisfactory.

Why was so little of a tangible nature accomplished despite the investment of so much? Many of the explanations that are customarily advanced are plausible, though not satisfactory. It may be argued that three years do not provide sufficient time to make significant changes in the policies of formal organizations, although the policies of complex national institutions are often changed through deliberate, calculated efforts within the same span of time. It is sometimes maintained that the resources for such social planning efforts are not adequate; but the record of the Ford Foundation projects suggests that misapplication of many available resources rather than limitations in supply more adequately explains the results. The limited accomplishments of these projects might be attributed to the ineptness and ignorance of the planners; yet the project directors were all well-trained and quite experienced. A comparison of the records of these planners with those of personnel in similar positions and activities suggests that in qualifications, experience, and previous performance the Ford project directors were better than average representatives of the professional men and women engaged in social planning and community organization. To be sure, their styles and preferences varied, and each of them worked in a somewhat different context of community resources and tradition; yet the results in each community were strikingly similar.

Much of the wasted effort in these projects is more satisfactorily accounted for by the lack of guides as to feasible undertakings. Without these guides it is understandable that the planners often persisted in attempts to achieve goals which violated the primary concerns of a target organization's policy faction, instead of recognizing the hopelessness of the situation and searching for different target organizations or suitable revisions which would have retained much, if not all, of the merit in their preference goals. Even when primary concerns were not violated, the lack of predictors as to open pathways hampered the planners in selecting appropriate resources for influence. Many resources were uselessly dissipated in situations where they could not be effective. Without a means for singling out the type of resources actually needed to overcome resistance to a particular goal, much time and energy were expended in indiscriminately acquiring a wide variety of resources in the hope that some of them might be useful. And in many instances, regardless of feasibility, it was not clear just how certain goals could be expected to bring about improvements in conditions of social welfare.

While the research necessary fully to comprehend planning as we have outlined it here has yet to be done, the perspective may, in itself, be immediately useful. Questions can be asked which may illuminate practical situations. Fresh approaches and a wider range of alternatives may be opened up. The situations confronted by planners in the Ford Foundation projects provide a convenient vehicle for applying some of the questions retrospectively to actual experience. Many may have been actually asked by the planner; if so, there is little indication that the implications generated were followed through to conclusions.

The San Francisco planner sought to establish a health screening service. Could this service be expected to improve the medical care received by elderly persons? Would engagement in a screening process bring about actual medical care for older persons not previously known to physicians? Would this enable participants to become patients of private physicians? Could the simple examination conducted in a screening process be expected to uncover a significant volume of hitherto unidentified health problems? Would results simply be recorded and filed away? Are other tested methods preferable for assuring that persons not under active medical supervision receive the care which they require? Answers to many of these questions are available in published reports and studies on programs of medical care.

The planner decided to build the screening program with contributions from the municipal health department and the local medical society. Is this likely to be a workable combination of participating organizations, given the traditions and background of cooperation and coordination in San Francisco? Will the proposed program violate the primary concerns of the dominant faction in either organization? If so, is it possible to find a different program proposal which would accomplish much the same purpose, but not violate these concerns? Are there other organizations which could be suitable targets for the same proposal? The past record of the health department's, the medical society's, and other organizations' responses to similar proposals should provide some clues.

The planner chose to maintain the initial preference goal and sought resources which might enable him to overcome anticipated resistance: five physicians in private practice and one of the grant programs of the U.S. Public Health Service. Could these physicians be expected to support the full screening program, as proposed? Would other resources be more committed and require less goal reduction to gain their participation? Could the physicians or others actually be influential in overcoming the resistance of the target organizations? What pathways are open for influencing the medical society and the health department? To what kinds of influence will they respond? Are the resources at hand useful on these pathways? If not, can the needed type of resources for influence be acquired elsewhere?

With the advantages of hindsight it seems relatively clear that the planning effort for a health screening program, as designed and carried out, was predestined to fail. The proposed program violated the primary concerns of one of the target organizations, and had to be drastically reduced in order to open any pathways. This reduction meant a virtual abandonment of the initial preference. The alternative of directing the goal toward other targets was not without promise, but the planner's efforts were invested in an attempt to overcome the resistance of the medical society. None of the available resources was helpful for this purpose, and it is not at all clear that others which might have been acquired would have been any more useful.

This series of questions can be similarly applied to each of the goals in the various projects. The appropriate questions might be particularly useful for planners to consider at certain critical stages in their planning efforts. When the Denver planner determined to convene a chronic-illness conference group comprised of forty-five agencies, for example, he might have asked himself: What should be the end product? Can forty-five agencies be expected to establish a workable program for coordinating all efforts? Where would the resources for such a program come from? Would a program actually emerge from a series of convocations, or would some specific proposals have to be introduced?

The need for a consideration of certain questions arose in Worcester half way through the planner's effort to establish a multiservice center when one of the target organizations was confronted with a crisis. The housing authority was subjected to a series of attacks by the city council. Did these attacks open up a pathway for influencing the authority to make a housing project site available for the center? If any, which one? Would it be more useful to support the authority during this crisis in order to open a different pathway on which the planner's resources could be effectively applied?

Questions like these can help planners to identify and establish feasible goals, reflecting the relevant variables in complex relationships between resistance and influence, and to clarify alternative courses of action. When further research is able to provide firm answers, selection and management of planning resources for improvements in social welfare will be even more effective. With an increase in our understanding of the cause-effect relations of changes in the policies of organizations, social planning can achieve far more in behalf of man's welfare.

VIII · BEYOND FEASIBILITY

Questions concerned with the balance between resistance and influence not only are helpful in identifying and establishing feasible goals, but also provide guidance for other steps necessary to bring planning endeavors to a successful conclusion. Even if a planner can establish a feasible situation, with an open pathway and suitable resources, he still needs to negotiate the path skillfully in order actually to overcome resistance and achieve his goal.

The dimensions of feasibility in a given situation will rather clearly indicate the major strategy that will have to be employed. If the planner needs to use resources for inducement, offering commodities that the target organization would like to acquire, then his basic strategy will be one of bargaining. A relatively stable relationship for negotiation is required in which the two parties can communicate about the terms of exchange. The planner's skill in these negotiations will determine just how much of the desired policy change he will obtain at the price he is able to offer.

The Worcester planner tried to induce the Bay State Rehabilitation Society to sponsor and administer a long-term program of recreational therapy in five local nursing homes. The inducements he offered were: a chance for the Society to establish working relationships with nursing homes (which it had been seeking for some time); provision of personnel and overhead costs involved in the proposal; and possible membership in, and financial support from, the Golden Rule Fund. In return for these the Society agreed to supervise the recreational therapist for one year, and to allow the use of its name in connection with the program.

In a different situation, the Contra Costa planner was able to get precisely what she wanted from a municipal housing authority. By offering the political support of a number of members of her planning committee, she induced the authority to submit a proposition for the construction of low-cost housing for the elderly to referendum. On another occasion, however, she was unable to get anything. She approached several agencies with an offer to show them how to run a recreational program if they would sponsor one, but this did not move them from their indifference.

When planner and target organization are seeking virtually the same specific ends, the basic strategy is cooperation. A relationship required for cooperative determinations is a firmly established pattern of communication. This pattern need not be formalized through official procedures and records, but can be an informal association involving periodic intercourse. Cooperation does not require a material exchange between parties. But, as in bargaining, however, both parties can gain if they pool their resources to achieve mutually satisfactory objectives. "Cooperative" meetings called when the parties do not genuinely share the same specific objectives are unlikely to result in cooperative pooling of assets. Forty-five organizations were brought together by the Denver planner in the hope that they would combine their resources. But this chronic-illness conference group achieved no concrete objective because there was little agreement as to specific ends. On the other hand, cooperation was possible between the Contra Costa planner and the county health officer because each was specifically interested in meeting the needs of chronically ill older persons, in finding a concrete program for doing so, and in establishing a new agency rather than relying upon existing programs.

When the planner cannot acquire tempting resources to offer a target organization and the two parties are relatively far apart in their purposes, the only strategy open to the planner, if he wishes to pursue his preference goal, is to engage in conflict. The central means for prevailing in conflict is, of course, coercion. But this is rarely a course of action available to social planners or desired by them. Usually, when planners do engage in conflict, it is by protesting or by stopping the flow of expected resources. In protesting either publicly or directly to the target organization the planner can sometimes create a nuisance. If the target organization is sufficiently bothered, it may make a change desired by the planner in order to get him to cease.[1]

This was a strategy often resorted to in Worcester. The planner's committee chairman attacked the housing authority at a public hearing before the city council, and his continuing pressure through statements to the newspapers and at various meetings and conferences probably played some part in the authority's subsequent decision to build a downtown project for the elderly and to increase the number of units planned.

None of the planners in the Ford Foundation projects was in a position to interrupt a flow of expected resources. But occasionally they were the objects of this strategy when it was employed by other planners. The director of Community Services in Worcester threatened to cut off the Golden Rule Fund's customary allocation for the Information Service for the Aged, which was being used as a nucleus for the projected multiservice center. In so doing, he hoped to forestall development of the center. In Contra Costa the director of the Council of Community Services objected to the planner's attempts to establish a new agency for homemaker and home nursing services. He disbanded the committee which the planner expected to pro-

---

[1] In effect, the planner's power to stop the nuisance places him in a bargaining position. See Wilson, "The Strategy of Protest: Problems of Negro Civic Action," *Journal of Conflict Resolution*, V (1961), 291–303.

vide an appropriate auspice for a project grant from the U.S. Public Health Service.

Protest may become an increasingly important strategy in social planning as more and more consumer groups organize to express their interests. The trend may go beyond the familiar phenomena of consumer cooperatives and the pooling of consumer purchasing power in health insurance organizations. American social welfare is currently undertaking experiments in getting the recipients of health and welfare services to be aware of their positions as consumers, and in organizing them to express their interests and rights as consumers.[2] If these experiments in organizing protest prove successful, such groups may become at specific times, and for certain purposes, the dominant factions of target organizations.

In addition to indicating the major strategy that a planner will have to undertake, attention to resistance and influence also brings to the fore several hazards which a planner will encounter as he attempts to negotiate his pathway successfully. One problem is the planner's temptation to invest energies along a number of fronts so he can feel certain that he is doing "all he can." The hazard here is a lack of time to think through any one approach with sufficient thoroughness to be effective. While each activity might be justified in some sense, the sum total of achievements may well be negligible. Each of the nearly thirty committees in San Francisco was devoted to a worthwhile purpose, but the project director spent most of her time scheduling, attending, and recording minutes of meetings. In Denver the planner extricated himself from this kind of difficulty when he recognized that his administration of the senior clubs' recreation programs was leaving him little time to plot his efforts carefully in order to achieve other, more important goals.

[2] See Sherrard and Murray, "The Church and Neighborhood Community," *Social Work*, X, No. 3 (1965), 3–14; Miller and Rein, "Will the War on Poverty Change America?" *Trans-Action*, II, No. 5 (1965), 17–23.

Another hazard to which a planner can be sensitive is competition from persons within his own organization. While resources are scarce, and strong competition is inevitable, it is sometimes possible to head off the competing demands of an ally. In Worcester, for example, both the planner and the executive of his organization wanted to get the use of a site in a public housing facility, in order to provide social services to tenants. The planner wanted the site for services to the elderly; unknown to him was his superior's intention to secure the location for work with younger families. Their competitive demands made it much more difficult for either of them to achieve their objectives.

Still another hazard is overeagerness to acquire a resource when a patiently plotted campaign may be needed in order to secure it. Frequently a suitable resource can only be obtained through a series of limited, carefully selected steps. A planner who begins with just his energy and expertness can often build upon these to obtain the aid of useful resources. These, in turn, can be used to attract still others. Through a series of such steps, the planner may be able to build a ladder which will put him in reach of the kinds of resources he requires for his immediate use. The Contra Costa planner, for example, needed funds to support a new county-wide agency. Although the California department of public health seemed a promising source of a demonstration grant, she did not approach it immediately. Her first step was to get the interest and support of the county health officer. Together they were able to assemble a committee composed of representatives from many of the private health agencies in the county. In due course, this committee won the favorable attention and support of several county governmental agencies. It also overcame opposition within the board of the Council of Community Services and gained its support. Now the planner felt that she was in a strong enough position to approach the state health department, and she was able to obtain a grant. In contrast, in Denver the planner made an early approach to the U.S. Public Health Service, requesting a "preplanning" grant to explore measures for coping with chronic illness among older persons. His proposal, unsupported by influential and representative spokesmen from the community, was rejected. Though interest in attaining such a grant was sustained for some time, all subsequent efforts were unsuccessful.

A premature attempt to secure an essential resource which is far out of reach may spoil a chance subsequently to build a ladder. Moreover, while quick results may be possible through reliance upon those resources which are easily and swiftly procured, this approach tends to blind a planner to opportunities for greater achievements. Swift, relatively minor successes may preclude the planner from ever undertaking the patient, delicate nurturing which is often required to obtain the resources essential for significant achievements. This is understandable in view of the many demands upon the planners, and the pressure for quick, visible results. The San Francisco project had an early success in forestalling the state proposal to reduce the rate of reimbursements to nursing homes. Yet no attempt was made to gain further ground in improving nursing home care, by building upon the interest and commitment of the persons and organizations involved in this early venture.

One more hazard worth mentioning is the kind of situation in which resources for influence have contradictory effects, canceling each other out. This usually happens when a planner is unable to control activities within his own organization, due to circumstances established prior to his employment. While the planner is trying to influence a target organization on one pathway, one of his associates may undermine him by trying another, simultaneous approach. The Worcester planner was continually attempting to overcome the resistance of the United Fund and the Planning Council by recruiting members

of the Yankee elite to his cause. But at the same time, his committee chairman was alienating this coterie by berating many
persons for their failure to recognize the multiservice center as
a worthwhile project. He antagonized a number of persons who
had been recruited by the planner and were actively engaged
in supporting his work: the vice-president of a major insurance
company, the president of the local medical society, a bank
president, the manager of a major local radio station, and many
others.

SOCIAL PLANNING IN TRANSITION

A generation and more ago financial support for social planning was provided primarily by local governments, philanthro-
pists, and businesses. But in the past thirty years private foundations and the federal government have come to provide an
overwhelming proportion of the funds expended in health and
welfare activity in all sectors of our society. Public sources currently account for about 85 percent of all expenditures for
income maintenance and welfare programs; prior to the pas-
sage of Medicare public expenditures in health and medical
care amounted to over $9 billion while private philanthropy
contributed some $848 million annually.[3] The Ford, Rocke-
feller, Commonwealth, Kellogg, Field, and some six thousand
other foundations now contribute a total of about $55 million a
year for health and welfare research purposes alone.[4]

One result of this trend is that the knowledge of many local
planners as to where, when, how, and for what they can obtain
financial resources is severely dated. The number and variety
of sources has increased enormously. Their interests and grant-
ing procedures are exceedingly varied and complex. Locally

[3] Merriam, "Social Welfare Expenditures 1963–64," *Social Security Bulletin*,
XXVII, No. 10 (1964), 3–14.
[4] A total of 6,007 foundations of varying size made health and welfare grants
in excess of $186 million a year. See *The Foundation Directory*.

based planners are often well acquainted with community resources and the purposes and conditions for obtaining them. For the most part, however, they have not yet acquired sufficient knowledge about national and state resources to regard them as "within ready reach." Many planners spend large proportions of their time and effort vaguely groping for clues as to remotely possible sources of support. Even when they find a suitable funding organization, they are often unable to tap the full opportunities presented. When contact is established, the local planner is often hindered by his lack of familiarity with the procedures, outlook, and criteria for evaluation operative in a given foundation or governmental unit. (Despite these difficulties the Ford project directors were able to tap some of these sources for funds useful in achieving several goals: for home care services in Contra Costa; for a consultation and referral service for the chronically ill in Denver; for a multiservice center for the aging in Worcester.)

It seems inevitable that the funds for major innovations in social welfare programs and services for many years to come will be provided mostly from sources that are not part of the traditional network of community welfare organizations. Local planners will need to become intimately acquainted with the identities, procedures, interests, and peculiarities of a myriad of foundations and public agencies. They may be helped by some developments of formal information systems regarding national resources of this character.

The major concerns of this volume have been the relevant variables for effective social planning. Only one type of planning has been considered in detail: feasible efforts to improve conditions of social welfare by changing the policies of organizations. This and other types of planning require further attention and understanding if professional practitioners are to have adequate technical skills for coping with social conditions. But as our discussion of financial trends has implied, many of the issues lying "beyond feasibility" deserve equal or greater attention within the larger context of the major developments in our society. The changes to be accomplished through improvements in professional practice are negligible in comparison with the challenges posed by emergent industrial, social, and political forces in American life. Our growing collective determination to respond to these forces must be buttressed by gigantic gains in knowledge and political sophistication. In the last analysis, vigorous advocacy, bold policy, and substantial support for creative research are our most effective resources for improving conditions of social welfare through planning. Even so, it is also clear that the technological challenges of coping with social problems in the twentieth century will require social planners who have sharpened their professional competence and skill.

BIBLIOGRAPHY

Bachrach, Peter, and Morton S. Baratz. "Two Faces of Power," *American Political Science Review*, LVI (1962), 947–52.

Banfield, Edward C. Political Influence. New York, Free Press of Glencoe, 1961.

—— "The Decision-making Schema," *Public Administration Review*, XVII (1957), 278–85.

—— "Does Consumers' Freedom Need Redefining?" Paper delivered at Brandeis University in the Colloquium Series of the Florence Heller Graduate School for Advanced Studies in Social Welfare, March, 1965.

Barnard, Chester. The Functions of the Executive. Cambridge, Mass., Harvard University Press, 1938.

Bell, Daniel. "Twelve Modes of Prediction," *Dædalus*, XCIII (1964), 845–80.

Billingsley, Andrew. The Role of the Social Worker in a Child Protective Agency. Boston, Society for the Prevention of Cruelty to Children, 1964.

Binstock, Robert H. "Demonstration-Research in the Planning of Services for the Elderly: an Analysis of Social Agency Project Sponsorship," in Eugene A. Friedmann and David Barkley, eds., The Uses of Research: a Report on the Applications of Research in Gerontology. Washington, D.C., United States Public Health Service, forthcoming, 1966.

—— "Determination, Equipment, and Strategic Position." Paper delivered at University of Michigan Conference on Aging, July, 1964.

Braybrooke, David. "The Mystery of Executive Success Re-examined," *Administrative Science Quarterly*, VIII (1964), 533–60.

Braybrooke, David, and Charles E. Lindblom. A Strategy of Decision: Policy Evaluation as a Social Process. New York, Free Press of Glencoe, 1963.

Clark, Peter B., and James Q. Wilson. "Incentive Systems: a Theory of Organizations," *Administrative Science Quarterly*, VI (1961), 129–66.

Dahl, Robert A. "The Analysis of Influence in Local Communities," in Charles R. Adrian, ed., Social Science and Community Action. Lansing, Michigan State University, 1960.

—— Who Governs? New Haven, Yale University Press, 1961.

Dahl, Robert A., and Charles E. Lindblom. Politics, Economics, and Welfare. New York, Harper & Brothers, Torchbook ed., 1963.

Deutsch, Karl W., and Leroy N. Rieselbach. "Recent Trends in Political Theory and Political Philosophy," *Annals*, CCCLX (1965), 139–62.

Foundation Library Center. The Foundation Directory, Edition 2. New York, Russell Sage Foundation, 1964.

Gouldner, Alvin. "The Secrets of Organizations," in *The Social Welfare Forum, 1963*. New York, Columbia University Press, 1963.

Halévy, Elie. The Growth of Philosophic Radicalism. Boston, Beacon Press, 1955.

Harrell, C. A., and D. G. Weiford. "The City Manager and the Policy Process," *Public Administration Review*, XIX (1959), 101–07.

Hollingshead, August B., and Frederick C. Redlich. Social Class and Mental Illness: a Community Study. New York, John Wiley and Sons, 1958.

de Jouvenel, Bertrand. On Power. New York, Viking Press, 1949.

Klein, Phillip. "The Social Theory of Professional Social Work," in Harry Elmer Barnes, Howard Becker, and Frances Bennett Becker, eds., Contemporary Social Theory. New York, D. Appleton Century, 1940.

Kravitz, Sanford. "Sources of Leadership Input for Social Welfare Planning." Unpublished doctoral dissertation, the Florence Heller Graduate School for Advanced Studies in Social Welfare, Brandeis University, 1963.

Mannheim, Karl. Man and Society in an Age of Reconstruction. New York, Harcourt, Brace and Company, 1940.

March, James G., and Herbert A. Simon. Organizations. New York, John Wiley and Sons, Inc., 1958.

Marschak, Jacob. "Efficient and Viable Organizational Forms," in

Mason Haire, ed., Modern Organizational Theory. New York, John Wiley and Sons, Inc., 1959.

May, Ernest R. "The Nature of Foreign Policy: the Calculated versus the Axiomatic," *Dædalus*, XCI (1962), 653–67.

Merriam, Ida C. "Social Welfare Expenditures, 1963–64." *Social Security Bulletin*, XXVII, No. 10 (1964), 3–14.

Meyerson, Martin. "The Utopian Tradition and the Planning of Cities," *Dædalus*, XC (1961), 180–93.

Michels, Robert. Political Parties. New York, Dover Publications, Inc., 1959.

Miller, S. Michael, and Martin Rein. "Will the War on Poverty Change America?" *Trans-Action*, II, No. 5 (1965), 17–23.

Morgan, James M., and others. Income and Welfare in the United States. New York, McGraw-Hill Book Company, 1962.

National Health Survey. Duration of Limitations of Activity Due to Chronic Conditions, United States, July 1959–June 1960. Washington, D.C., United States Public Health Service Publication No. 584–B31, 1962.

Peterson, Lorin. The Day of the Mugwump. New York, Random House, 1961.

Polsby, Nelson W. Community Power and Political Theory. New Haven, Yale University Press, 1963.

Price, Don K. "The Promotion of the City Manager Plan," *Public Opinion Quarterly*, V (1941), 563–78.

Randall, Ollie A., and Robert Morris. "Planning and Organization of Community Services for the Elderly," *Social Work*, X, No. 1 (1965), 96–102.

Ross, Murray G. Community Organization. New York, Harper and Brothers, 1955.

Ross, Murray G., and Charles E. Hendry. New Understandings of Leadership. New York, Association Press, 1957.

Rossi, Peter H., and Robert Dentler. The Politics of Urban Renewal. Glencoe, Ill., Free Press, 1961.

Schorr, Alvin. Filial Responsibility in the Modern American Family. Washington, D.C., United States Department of Health, Education, and Welfare, 1960.

Schottland, Charles I. "Federal Planning for Health and Welfare," in *The Social Welfare Forum, 1963*. New York, Columbia University Press, 1963.

Seeley, John R. "Central Planning: Prologue to a Critique," in
Robert Morris, ed., Centrally Planned Change. New York, National Association of Social Workers, 1964.

Sherrard, Thomas B., and Richard C. Murray. "The Church and
Neighborhood Community Organizations," Social Work, X, No.
3 (1965), 3–14.

Simon, Herbert A. Administrative Behavior: a Study of Decision-
making Processes in Administrative Organizations. New York,
Macmillan, 1957.

—— Models of Man: Social and Rational. New York, John Wiley
and Sons, Inc., 1957.

—— "On the Concept of Organizational Goal," Administrative
Science Quarterly, IX (1964), 1–22.

Simon, Herbert A., Donald W. Smithburg, and Victor A. Thompson.
Public Administration. New York, Alfred A. Knopf, 1961.

Snow, C. P. The Masters. New York, Doubleday and Company,
1959.

"Social Programs through Social Planning: the Role of Social
Work." Report of the Pre-Conference Working Party to the
Twelfth International Conference of Social Work. Chalkis,
Greece, International Conference of Social Work, 1965.

Somers, Herman M., and Anne R. Somers. Doctors, Patients, and
Health Insurance. Garden City, N.Y., Doubleday and Company,
Anchor ed., 1961.

Srole, Leo, and others. Mental Health in the Metropolis. New York,
McGraw-Hill Book Company, 1962.

Taber, Merlin, Franz Itzin, and William Turner. Comparative Analysis of Health and Welfare Service in One County. Iowa City,
Institute of Gerontology, State University of Iowa, 1963.

Tibbits, Clark, ed. Handbook of Social Gerontology. Chicago, University of Chicago Press, 1960.

Titmuss, Richard M. "Social Administration in a Changing Society,"
in Essays on the Welfare State. New Haven, Yale University
Press, 1959.

United States Census, 1950 and 1960.

Vinter, Robert. "Analysis of Treatment Organizations," Social Work,
VIII, No. 3 (1963), 3–15.

Weiner, Hyman J. "Toward Techniques for Social Change," Social
Work, VI, No. 2 (1961), 26–35.

White House Conference on Aging. The Nation and Its Older

People. Washington, D.C., United States Department of Health, Education, and Welfare, 1961.

Whyte, William F. Street Corner Society. Chicago, University of Chicago Press, 1943.

Wickenden, Elizabeth. "Social Action," in Encyclopedia of Social Work. New York, National Association of Social Workers, 1965.

Wilson, James Q. "An Overview of Theories of Planned Change," in Robert Morris, ed., Centrally Planned Change. New York, National Association of Social Workers, 1964.

—— "The Strategy of Protest: Problems of Negro Civic Action," *Journal of Conflict Resolution*, V (1961), 291–303.

INDEX

Adult Education Association (Denver), 62
Age Center of Worcester Area, 74-76
Aging: *see* Older persons
Allied Jewish Council (Denver), 62
American Red Cross: San Francisco, 40, 41; Contra Costa County, 51, 121

Bachrach, Peter, 18n-19n
Banfield, Edward C., 18, 77-78, 109n, 113-114n, 115n, 116n, 117
Baratz, Morton S., 18n-19n
Barnard, Chester, 106n, 119n
Bay Area Welfare Planning Federation (Calif.), 38
Bay Area Workshop (Calif.), 59
Bay State Rehabilitation Society (Worcester), 70, 150-51
Bell, Daniel, 9n
Bentham, Jeremy, 19
Billingsley, Andrew, 108n
Binstock, Robert H., 86n, 124n
Boston, 36
Braybrooke, David, 7n, 17n, 27n

California: population changes, 36; employment service, 42; department of finance, 47-48, 137; governor, 48, 137; Advisory Committee on Aging, 58; department of welfare, 58; department of health, 154-55
Canon Kip Community House (San Francisco), 42
Casework services for the elderly: in San Francisco, 39, 40-41, 123-24, 130, 131-32, 142; in Denver, 62, 143; in Worcester, 70-71, 143; in Contra Costa County, 142

Catholic Committee for the Aging (San Francisco), 43
Centers for the elderly: multiservice center in Worcester, 70-76, 100-101, 120, 123, 126, 130-31, 133-34, 136-39, 143, 152, 156, 157; *see also* Recreation programs for the elderly
Chronic Illness Service Center (San Francisco), 39
Chronic illness service programs: in San Francisco, 39, 41, 45-47, 83, 96-97, 111-12, 119-20, 125, 135-36, 146-48; in Denver, 61, 64-67, 99-100, 134, 142-43, 148, 151, 154, 157; mentioned, 10, 34; *see also* Home care services for the elderly
City planning, 8, 13
Clark, Peter B., 106, 107
Colorado: role in field of aging, 59; Governor's Commission on Aging, 62; department of health, 66
Colorado Tuberculosis Association, 66
Commonwealth Foundation, 156
Community Chest and Council (Worcester), 69
Community Facilities Act, 54
Community organization, 3, 15-16
Community planning, 15-16
Community power, 18-19
Community Services of Greater Worcester: Golden Rule Fund, 37, 69-72, 74-76, 100-101, 120, 123, 136-37, 150-51, 152, 155; Planning Council, 70-72, 74-76, 100-101, 114, 123, 133-34, 136-37, 155
Conference Group on Chronic Disease and Rehabilitation (Denver), 65-66, 99-100, 120, 148, 151

Conference of Nonprofit Housing for the Aging (Denver), 67-68, 138-39

Contra Costa Committee on Aging: general description, 50-53; goals, 50-52; leadership for planning, 52-53, 125-126; health planning, 53-56, 97-98, 120, 151, 152-53, 154, 157; housing planning, 56-57, 83, 98-99, 120, 151; recreation planning, 57-59; friendly visiting program, 121; achievements, 142

Contra Costa Council of Community Services, 50-52, 54, 55, 56, 98, 125, 152-53, 154

Contra Costa County (Calif.): as site of demonstration project, 32, 35, 82, 125-26, 151, 152, 154, 157; selective description, 36-37, 49-59 passim, 97-99; welfare department, 49, 53, 97-98, 114, 120; hospital, 49, 53, 98; health department, 49, 53, 55, 98; heart association, 53, 98; cancer association, 53, 98; housing authority, 57, 99, 120; medical society, 98

Contra Costa County Board of Supervisors, 55

Council of Churches (San Francisco), 43, 45

Dahl, Robert A., 5, 18n, 114n, 115n, 116n, 123n

Dentler, Robert, 3n

Denver: as site of demonstration project, 32, 35, 82, 83, 99-100, 120, 134-35, 138-39, 148, 151, 153, 154, 157; selective description, 36-37, 59-69 passim; Mayor's Commission on Aging, 59, 62; housing authority, 61; department of parks and recreation, 62, 68-69, 99

Denver Area Welfare Council, 59-60

Deutsch, Karl W., 94n

Economic Opportunity Program, 90

Elderly: see Casework services for the elderly; Centers for the elderly; Chronic illness service programs; Employment programs for the elderly; Friendly-visiting programs for the elderly; Home care services for the elderly; Hospitalization of the elderly; Housing for the elderly; Income maintenance for the elderly; Information and referral programs for the elderly; Older persons; Recreation programs for the elderly; Retirement preparation programs; Service programs for the elderly

Employment programs for the elderly: in San Francisco, 42, 142; in Contra Costa County, 142

Family Service Agency (San Francisco), 40

Family Service Association of America, 109n

Family Service Organization (Worcester), 70-71

Field Foundation, 156

Fitch, Lyle C., 78

Florence Heller Graduate School for Advanced Studies in Social Welfare, Brandeis University, 32n

Ford Foundation: as sponsor of demonstration-research program, 32, 33, 35-77 passim, 83, 97, 111-12, 119, 121, 122, 123, 134, 137, 141-42, 144-46, 152, 157; general role in field of aging, 33, 35; mentioned, 156

Friendly visiting programs for the elderly: in San Francisco, 41, 142; in Contra Costa County, 51, 121, 142; in Worcester, 71

Goals: general meaning, 5, 80; value preference in, 21-22; difficulty of distinguishing from means, 22-23; type considered here, 23-24; of San Francisco demonstration project, 40-42; of Contra Costa County demonstration project, 50-52; of Denver demonstration project, 61-62; of Worcester demonstration project, 70-71; haphazard emergence of, 76-79; as solutions to problems of social welfare, 86-93, 95; see also Preference goals

Golden Years, Inc. (Marion Co., Kans.), 32n

Gouldner, Alvin, 78

Halévy, Elie, 19n

Harrell, C. A., 107n

Health and Welfare Council of Metropolitan St. Louis, 32n

Hendry, Charles E., 106n

Hollingshead, August B., 90n

Home care services for the elderly: in San Francisco, 41; in Contra Costa County, 51, 53-56, 97-98, 142, 151, 152-53, 157; in Denver, 143; mentioned, 10, 35

Hospitalization of the elderly: in Worcester, 69, 82; in Contra Costa County, 82; mentioned, 34-35

Housing for the elderly: in San Francisco, 42; in Contra Costa County, 51, 56-57, 83, 98-99, 120, 142, 151; in Denver, 61, 67-68, 138-39, 142; in Worcester, 71, 101, 120, 143, 148, 152; mentioned, 10, 22

Income maintenance for the elderly, 10, 59

Influence: defined, 18, 113; organizational responsiveness to, 30-31, 110-41 *passim;* general relevance for social planning, 113–15; difficulties of identifying, 116; "pathways" of, 116-18; potential resources for, 118-19; availability of resources for, 119, 121-41 *passim;* acquisition of resources for, 123-26, 129, 132-38, 154-57

Information and referral programs for the elderly: in San Francisco, 42, 44-45, 142; in Worcester, 69, 71, 152

Information Service for the Aging (Worcester), 69, 71, 152

Itzin, Frank, 90n

Jewish Community Center (San Francisco), 43

Jewish Family Service: San Francisco, 40; Worcester, 70

Jouvenel, Bertrand de, 18n

Junior League: Contra Costa County, 53; Worcester, 74-75, 101

Kellogg Foundation, 156

Klein, Phillip, 88

Kravitz, Sanford, 40n

Langley Porter Neuropsychiatric Clinic (San Francisco), 45

Lindblom, Charles E., 5, 7n, 27n

Mannheim, Karl, 8n, 11

March, James G., 94-95, 102, 103, 139

Marion County (Kans.), 32n

Marschak, Jacob, 86n

Martinez (Calif.): potential site for public housing construction, 51, 57

Massachusetts: department of welfare, 70; department of health, 75

May, Ernest R., 87n

MCCS: *see* Metropolitan Council for Community Service

Merriam, Ida C., 156n

Metropolitan Council for Community Service (Denver), 5, 59-64, 66, 68, 82, 83, 135

Metropolitan Planning Project for Older People (Denver): general description, 59, 62; goals, 61-62; planning arrangements, 61-64, 83-84, 135; health planning, 64-67, 99-100, 120, 134, 148, 151, 154, 157; housing planning, 67-68, 138-39; recreation planning, 68-69, 99, 120, 153; achievements, 143

Meyerson, Martin, 19n

Michels, Robert, 103n

Mile High Fund (Denver): funds raised per capita, 37; relationship with MCCS, 61, 63, 64, 82

Miller, S. Michael, 153n

Minnesota, 32n

Morgan, James M., 90n, 91n

Morris, Robert, 124n, 133n

MPPOP: *see* Metropolitan Planning Project for Older People

Murray, Richard C., 153n

National Annuity League, 59

National Council on the Aging, 35, 57, 68

Nursing homes: in San Francisco, 41, 47-48, 137, 142; in Denver, 62; in Worcester, 70, 121, 143, 150-51; mentioned, 10, 35

Office of Manpower, Automation, and Training (U.S.), 42

Older persons: general programs and services for, 9-11; increased longevity in U.S., 33; problems confronted by, 33-35, 87, 88, 90; proportion in Worcester, 37; proportion in San Francisco, 37; proportion in Contra Costa County, 37; proportion in Denver, 37

Organizations: as targets of planning, 14-15, 22-24, 25; as employers of planners, *see* Planner; goals of, 25-26, 103; tendency to resist planning goals, 28-31, 94-96, 102-03; policy determination within, 29-30, 140; decision-making in, 102-04; factions of, as targets for influence, 103-04, 110, 113-14, 118-41 *passim;* boards of directors, 104-06; executives, 107-08; staffs, 108; members and consumers, 109-10; defined, 119*n*; *see also* Influence

Peterson, Lorin, 3*n*
Planner: general meaning, 5; as defined here, 15-18, 119*n*; relationship with employer, 25, 119, 123-26, 128, 154, 155; influence possessed by, 27, 28-31, 118-41 *passim*
Planning: general meaning, 4-5, 7-9; limitations of present concepts, 6-7, 12-13; reasons for confusion about, 9-14; "social" types, 14-15; "social" type considered here, 15-24; as intervention for social welfare, 80-86; motives for, 84-86
Policy change: defined, 94
Polsby, Nelson W., 19*n*, 115*n*, 119*n*
Preference goals: defined, 27; as proposals for organizational policy change, 28, 94-96, 110-11, 113, 128-41 *passim;* functions of, 80; development of, as solutions to problems of social welfare, 86-93; revision of, 130-36; predicting feasibility of, 140-41
Price, Don K., 104*n*

Randall, Ollie A., 124*n*
Recreation programs for the elderly: in San Francisco, 41-44, 97; in Contra Costa County, 51-52, 57-59, 142, 151; in Denver, 62, 68-69, 99, 143, 153; in Worcester, 69-70, 143, 150-51; mentioned, 10-11; *see also* Centers for the elderly
Redlich, Frederick C., 90*n*
Rein, Martin, 153*n*
Retirement preparation programs: in San Francisco, 42; in Denver, 62, 143; mentioned, 10

Richmond (Calif.): potential site for public housing construction, 51, 56; housing authority, 56, 58, 98-99; city council, 56, 58; recreation department, 58; recreation center, 58-59
Rieselbach, Leroy N., 94*n*
Rockefeller Foundation, 156
Ross, Murray G., 3*n*, 16*n*, 106*n*
Rossi, Peter H., 3*n*

St. Louis, 32*n*
Salvation Army: San Francisco, 45; Worcester, 70, 72-73, 126, 139
San Francisco: as site of demonstration project, 32, 35, 111-12, 119, 123-24, 125, 130, 131, 135-37, 146-47, 153, 155; selective description, 36-48 *passim,* 96-97, 111-12; Mayor's Commission on Aging, 38; department of welfare, 41, 46, 123-24; department of health, 41, 46, 96, 135, 147; department of recreation, 41, 43; public library, 41, 97; redevelopment authority, 42; housing authority, 42; mayor, 124
San Francisco Central Labor Union, 48, 137
San Francisco Hotel Association, 42, 45
San Francisco Medical Society, 41, 46, 47, 96-97, 111-12, 114, 119, 136, 147
San Francisco Program for the Aging: general description, 39-42, 153; goals, 40-42; recreation planning, 42-45, 97, 120; health planning, 45-48, 83, 96-97, 111-12, 119-20, 125, 135, 136, 137, 146-47, 155; casework planning, 123-24, 130, 131-32; achievements, 142
San Pablo (Calif.): potential site for public housing construction, 56; housing authority, 56, 98-99; city council, 56
SCC: *see* Senior Citizens' Council
Schorr, Alvin, 35*n*
Schottland, Charles I., 6
Seeley, John R., 78
Senior citizens' centers: *see* Recreation programs for the elderly
Senior Citizens' Council (Denver), 59-64, 68, 82, 135

Senior citizens' groups: see Recreation programs for the elderly
Sherrard, Thomas B., 153n
Simon, Herbert A., 77, 86n, 94-95, 102, 103, 106n, 139
Smithburg, Donald W., 95
Snow, C. P., 115n
Social welfare: defined, 19-22; financial trends in, 156-58
Somers, Anne R., 109n
Somers, Herman M., 109n
SPA: see San Francisco Program for the Aging
Srole, Lee, 90n
Strategies, 150-53

Taber, Merlin, 90n
Thompson, Victor A., 95
Tibbits, Clark, 33n
Titmuss, Richard M., 108n
Twelfth International Conference of Social Work, 5-6
Turner, William, 90n

United Bay Area Crusade (Calif.): funds raised per capita, 37; comparative allocation of funds to San Francisco and Contra Costa County, 37, 50; relationship with United Community Fund of San Francisco, 38; relationship with West Contra Costa Community Welfare Council, 49; mentioned, 53
United Community Fund of San Francisco: as sponsor of demonstration project, 38-40; Social Planning Department, 38, 42, 45, 48, 124
United Community Funds and Councils of America, 36n
United States Public Health Service, 41, 47, 51, 54, 55, 66, 75-76, 98, 125, 134, 137, 147, 153, 154
University of California, 44
University of Denver, 67

Vinter, Robert, 88n

Visiting Nurse Association: San Francisco, 46; Contra Costa County, 97

WCA: see Worcester Committee on Aging
Weiford, D. G., 107n
Weiner, Hyman J., 108n
West Contra Costa Board of Realtors (Calif.), 98
West Contra Costa Community Welfare Council (Calif.), 49, 50, 52, 97
Western Geriatric Society (Colo.), 66
White House Conference on Aging 1961, 35, 63
Whyte, William F., 115n
Wickenden, Elizabeth, 3n
Wilson, James Q., 5, 27n, 106, 107, 152n
Worcester (Mass.): as site of demonstration project, 32, 35, 121, 123, 126, 130, 133, 136-3', 139, 148, 150, 152, 154, 155, 157; selective description, 36, 37, 69-76 passim, 100-101; department of welfare, 69-70; department of parks, 70, 73, 139; housing authority, 70, 71, 73, 101, 120, 130, 139, 152, 154; health department, 70; city manager, 75; need for services for the elderly, 81-82; city council, 152; medical society, 156
Worcester Committee on Aging: general description, 69-72; goals, 70-71; planning for a multiservice center for the elderly, 71-76, 100-101, 120, 123, 126, 130, 133-34, 136-37, 139, 148, 152, 154, 155-56, 157; housing planning, 101, 120, 148, 152; attempt to improve nursing home services, 121, 150-51; achievements, 142-43
Worcester Council of Churches, 75
Worcester State Hospital, 69, 82

YWCA: San Francisco, 45; Worcester, 69, 72, 74-76, 101, 130, 139; mentioned, 109n